CAN MY CHURCH GROW?

by
Martin Goldsmith

HODDER AND STOUGHTON
LONDON SYDNEY AUCKLAND TORONTO

Biblical quotations are taken from the Revised Standard Version.

British Library Cataloguing in Publication Data
Goldsmith, Martin
  Can my church grow?
  1. Church growth
  I. Title
  254   BV652.25

ISBN 0 340 25337 1

CAN MY CHURCH GROW?

CONTENTS

CAN MY CHURCH GROW?

1 CHURCHES SHOULD GROW

Christians in the western world face today a new and stimulating challenge. While the Churches of Africa, Asia and Latin America mushroom with new life, many of our own congregations have steadily declined during the past decades. A growing awareness of what is happening, coupled with a discontent at the present situation, is leading to a longing to recapture the fresh and adventurous faith of Christians overseas. No longer can we be complacent at the sight of half-empty old churches in our towns and cities. No longer are we satisfied with the miniscule congregations of many village churches. We have experienced the failure of joining one dying congregation with another equally moribund congregation in the hope that together they may evidence new life.

The glaring needs of new towns and housing areas challenge us to face their social problems and religious indifference. Maintaining a stagnant status quo can no longer satisfy.

Christians are beginning to realise how puny is the impact we make on society as a whole. We cannot expect our voice to be listened to when we form only a small minority of the local population. A congregation of two hundred Christians in a town of 10,000 people comprises only 2 per cent of the population and can only therefore be considered rather insignificant. In comparison with other churches with mere handfuls of attendants, we may feel that a congregation of two hundred is encouraging. We fail to see the reality of the situation when we only compare ourselves with other churches. It was stimulating recently to hear a vicar setting targets for realistic growth. He had realised that any society only makes a decisive impact when its membership forms at least 5 per cent of the local population.

The television screen dominates many homes. Social gossip centres on the previous evening's viewing. Mass media are today recognised as a key factor in the shaping of opinions and attitudes, but they pay scanty regard to active Christian faith at grass-roots level. Christians desperately need to influence the content of the mass media. A beginning has been made with the use of modern approaches. Christian pop festivals, drama groups and radio ministries have begun to compete for the hearts and minds of the younger generation. Much more needs to be done.

In various ways therefore the Christian Church is beginning to wake up from its slumbers and lethargic contentment with small and uninfluential congregations. We begin to see that we are missionaries here in the western world. We desire to grow. But this inevitably raises various problems. Perhaps the greatest deterrent to relevant evangelistic impact is our fear of alienating the traditional church-goer. Many a minister wonders how to make the Church and the Gospel attractive to the outsider without losing older and more traditional members. He may also be afraid of reducing his standards of worship and Bible teaching, and thus sacrificing quality for quantity. In many minds relevant evangelism is sadly associated with shallow gimmicry and personal growth in holiness considered almost incompatible with modern forms of outreach.

When Jesus summoned his disciples to follow him, he gave them complementary commands. The apparent passivity of "to be with him" matches the greater activism of being "sent out to preach" (Mark 3:14). Such balance eludes many Christians today. Some are characterised by a prayerful piety and deep holiness while others fervently fill their lives with zealous evangelism and ministry. The former impresses with his sanctity, but produces little fruit outside his own personal life. The latter gets results, but their shallowness may reflect his rootlessness. The Christian disciple is called to depth of worship and sanctification as well as to be out-going in evangelistic outreach.

This tension in the lives of individual disciples applies equally to the Church as a body. Edification of believers and evangelisation of the world should go together as a church's twin purposes. In healthy churches growth should be evidenced not only in quantity and quality, but also in structural organisation. These three should be continuous and simultaneous.

1 *Quantity*

Complacency ill befits a church which does not grow numerically. We cannot be content with the faithlessness reflected in such comments as "Praise God;

we're holding our own." The New Testament churches have given us a pattern whereby new members should be added regularly to the Church. The initial influx of about 3,000 new believers at Pentecost (Acts 2:42) led on to the Lord adding to their number day by day those who were being saved (Acts 2:43). As a result of this growth about 5,000 men joined the Church in Acts 4:4 and the story of Acts then shows the expansion of the Church around the Mediterranean. Some have criticised such insistence on numerical growth, saying that it glories in statistics without real personal concern for people. This is of course a danger, but statistics do portray God's dealings with men and women. If new members are not being added to the Church, it means that the wonder of life in Christ is not being imparted to outsiders who are therefore being allowed to remain "alienated … strangers to the covenant of promise, having no hope and without God in the world" (Eph. 2:12).

There are several forms of quantitative growth.

(a) *Biological growth* On visiting a church for the first time I often enquire about the life and progress of that church. Frequently the leaders of the congregation reply, "The Lord has really blessed us this past year we have had ten young people converted." Further conversation reveals that these conversions have mostly been among the children of Christian families. It is of course important that the life of the local congregation be of such a character that members' children are attracted to Christ and not put off by boring meetings or unloving inflexibility in the church. Winning children of believers to committed adult faith in Christ is not only vital for the numerical growth of the church, but also to prevent the tragedy and parental heartache which each "prodigal son" causes. Sadly our country is littered with those who have rejected the faith of their parents. Their lives testify to the failure of the Church to express the Gospel in meaningful terms.

In most Third World countries the population grows by about $2\frac{1}{2}$–3 per cent per annum. On the dual assumption that Christians are as productive as their non-Christian compatriots and that the Church includes people of all ages, the Church ought to grow by $2\frac{1}{2}$–3 per cent per annum even without winning any from outside the Christian community. If the Church remains static, merely "holding its own", this actually means that it is probably losing its young people.

Biological Church growth is extremely important, but we should also be bringing total non-Christians into the joy of salvation in Christ.

(b) *Transfer growth* The modern world is characterised by rapid urbanisation and increasing fluidity of society.

City churches will almost certainly gain from an inflow of Christians from country churches. They may often feel culturally disorientated in the bustle and sophistication of the metropolis. Many will not feel at home in the relatively large churches of the city. They may therefore be tempted to drop out from Christian worship and fellowship. The country church leaders need to give them introductions to sympathetic Christians in their new urban environment. Likewise the already established city congregation must go out of its way to welcome the newly arrived country brother.

In the fluid society of a modern State, Christians may

only stay in a church for a very few years before moving on to a new job in a new area. Research in an Anglican church in a small town north of London revealed that most members only stayed about four years before moving. This underlines the importance of integrating new members quickly into the life and ministry of the local congregation. Any church which lacks the necessary warm spontaneity will lose some of the possible transfer growth and will also find an increasingly large percentage of its laity remain peripheral to the Bible teaching and evangelistic ministry of the church.

In the modern world transfer growth is a vital component in the life of the church. But, as with biological growth, it cannot be sufficient in itself if the Church throughout the country is to grow. Evidence would seem to suggest that biological and transfer growth are better maintained if a congregation is also geared to the effective evangelisation of non-Christians. The church which attracts many non-Christians will probably find it easier to incorporate its own children and Christians from other areas. Churches which fail in their evangelistic task outside the Christian community will probably also lose many of their young people and a large portion of the possible transfer growth.

(c) *Conversion growth* In the following chapters of this book we shall talk in much greater detail about this, but we need at this stage to affirm that one vital function of the Christian Church is to preach the Gospel of Christ in the power and love of the Holy Spirit with the result that men and women turn to Jesus Christ and enter his Church. We long for multitudes to be converted and share with us the saving knowledge of the Lord. Conversion should automatically mean incorporation into the Church: it is never meant to be a merely individualistic relationship with God. Conversion includes being added to the Church and thus the Church grows.

This would all seem very obvious! It is however sometimes helpful to point out the significance of the obvious. Thus everybody knew that if someone gets into a full bath it will overflow. Archimedes merely pointed out the significance of the obvious. Likewise we did not need a Newton to teach us that ripe apples fall rather than ascend into heaven! What then is the significance of this obvious biblical truth that churches ought to grow through the winning of converts?

Many churches have so forgotten this primary fact that they can boast of their doctrinal integrity, their orderly church life and their regular evangelistic activities without realising that despite everything they are not growing. This does not seem to concern them. Likewise, some Missions seem to have become so engrossed in running their medical and educational work that they fail to observe their failure in the realm of church growth. Such social activities as medical and educational ministries have a validity of their own which none of us would wish to denigrate, but surely no Mission should be content if their work does not lead to the Church growing through the conversion of men and women. Extreme situations like some strictly Muslim lands may be exceptions to this general principle, but even then we long for people to come to faith in Christ even if they cannot openly be joined to the visible Christian Church.

2 *Quality*

In *Understanding Church Growth* Dr. McGavran emphasises that quantitative and qualitative growth should continue simultaneously in the life of the healthy Christian Church. He rejects the idea that a period of active and successful evangelism may then necessitate a time of consolidation before returning to evangelism again. Such a stop-go policy, he says, will lead to stagnation.

It is good for a congregation to have members at every stage of spiritual development. The newest converts with all their immaturity are often those who appeal most easily to the unconverted outsider, but the different ministries within the fellowship will also need more mature Christians who between them will be able to exercise a rich variety of gifts.

The New Testament clearly demonstrates God's desire that all of us should grow up into the full stature of Christ. New birth and the early enthusiasm of a young Christian delight us all, but we are saddened when we encounter Christians who over the years remain babes in Christ.

The Lord wants us to grow more like him in holiness of life. This will necessitate a growing personal relationship with him in Bible study, prayer and meditation. Such a relationship of love will inevitably move us to lives of obedience, for in the Bible we note that love and obedience walk hand in hand.

But our qualitative growth will not be only in terms of personal sanctification. It will also produce growth in our service for our neighbour. The command to love our neighbour as much as we love ourselves challenges us to dedicate ourselves to the promotion of others' welfare.

This will include a rich variety of social welfare activities, but may also push us into the world of economic and political structures which so influence the fate of us all. As Orlando Costas points out in *The Church and its Mission*, the Church Growth movement* is sometimes rather weak in respect to socio-political questions. It tends to emphasise the Great Commission above the Great Commandment to love our neighbour, whereas the two need to be kept together and equal.

To summarise, God looks for qualitative growth in personal sanctification, in relationship with the Lord and with our fellow Christians, and in our loving service to our neighbour.

3 *Structural growth*

Some evangelicals today react suspiciously to the whole concept of organisation. They are right to reject rigid structures which may quench the Spirit's spontaneous freedom. Freedom and flexibility will characterise any live church, but there is also need for such orderly structures and organisation as will facilitate the smooth running of the life of the Church.

A small family requires relatively little organisation in the home. Meals can be arranged with a minimum of planning whenever the two or three members of the family are hungry. But when the family increases to ten or fifteen people, planning and organisation must develop also. This truth applies equally to any institution.

---

*This movement which researches the growth of churches worldwide is centred on the Church Growth Institute at Fuller Theological Seminary, Pasadena, California. It was founded by Dr Donald McGavran.

A college with fifty students will not require the degree of efficient organisation that is needed in a college of 150 students. We sometimes forget the obvious relevance of this to the Christian Church. I remember a small Methodist church in Singapore where missionaries from the much larger American Methodist churches had imposed structures which were far too involved for a small congregation. As a result every active member was encumbered with manifold committees and bureaucratic functions. On the other hand some British missionaries have only been accustomed at home to little churches of 50–100 people at Sunday services. They do not know how to structure a congregation with 1,000 or 2,000 on an average Sunday morning. This problem afflicts various of our livelier churches even in the west. They have outgrown their organisational structures and therefore any further numerical growth would lead inevitably to a lack of fellowship within the body of believers and also to the breakdown of pastoral care. If numerical growth is to be accompanied by qualitative growth, it must also be matched by structural developments.

Pasadena and Europe learn from each other

This approach to growth is a basic tenet of the Church Growth movement. In theory then the movement teaches the necessity of progressive development along these three tracks simultaneously – quantity, quality and organisation. In practice however their materials tend to stress numerical growth almost to the exclusion of any interest in the sanctification and edification of believers. This over-emphasis is strongly rejected by Christian leaders who observe the scandal of the multiplication of untaught and unsanctified church members. Statistics of numerical growth may give a misleading impression of healthy and spiritual churches, whereas a closer knowledge of the situation may give reason for alarm. Sanctification is hard to plot on statistical graphs. On the other hand the churches in the west have often grown up in times when the whole nation was nominally Christian. They have tended therefore to become largely pastoral and Bible-teaching institutions with little idea how to evangelise largely irreligious populations. The function of the minister is seen primarily in terms of preaching and pastoral care within the congregation; rare indeed is the minister with evangelistic gifts. Church services and even mid-week home meetings are normally more suited to Christians than to people of little or no Christian background. Few church members enjoy the exciting privilege of leading people to personal faith in Christ; even fewer have caught the vision of planting new churches in unevangelised housing estates or de-Christianised villages. The western Church has often lost the vision for expansion and numerical growth in the Church. Of course it is true, as Pope Paul VI said in his apostolic exhortation *Evangelii Nuntiandi*, that "the Church is an evangeliser, but she begins by being evangelised herself". Karl Barth called this the Church's "ministry ad intra", but he too saw it as preliminary to the "ministry ad extra".

The Church Growth movement and the western churches have much to contribute to each other. For some years the criticisms from Europe have been penetrating the systems of Pasadena and now more recently the churches of Europe have begun to realise their need of the methodological challenges which their American friends deliver so pungently. Missionaries all over the world are today faced with Church Growth thinking and on return to their home countries they introduce it to churches and ministers who have not had the benefit of this wider experience. There remains one large hurdle. This movement is fundamentally very American and needs to be culturally and theologically adjusted if it is to take root in European soil.

Methodology or the Holy Spirit?

Perhaps the greatest cultural obstacle to Christians in Europe is the strong emphasis on methodology. They feel happier with the approach of Roland Allen in his classic book *Missionary Methods: St. Paul's or Ours?* in which he shows the patterns of missionary strategy in Paul's ministry, but nevertheless stresses the sovereign freedom and power of the Holy Spirit. In this respect it is interesting to compare the thinking of Roland Allen with that of Michael Green in his somewhat related book *Evangelism in the Early Church*. Both, in their very different ways, underline the missionary methods of the early apostles, but Allen has a greater emphasis on the Holy Spirit. Methodology without submission to the sovereignty of the Spirit is spiritually dangerous. The Book of Acts does unfold patterns of strategy which are important for us to learn, but the key to apostolic success was the life-giving power of the Spirit. H. Boer in *Pentecost and Missions* is surely right when he argues that mission is dependent on the pentecostal gift of the Spirit. Boer expounds the Genesis account of how God breathed into man's nostrils "the breath of life"

(Gen. 2:7) and sees an inevitable result that man should "be fruitful and multiply" (Gen. 1:28). Likewise Pentecost led directly to the multiplication of the early Church, and the continuing gift of the Holy Spirit throughout the Book of Acts always leads to multitudes being added to the Church.

We have been given brains to use for the Lord. We are expected in our church ministries to evaluate our strategies to the best of our ability. Trust in the Spirit is not blind. But our human attempts to formulate right missionary policies and approaches are always to be subject to God's Spirit. His ways are sometimes not our ways. Thus in Acts 8 it must have seemed to Philip that God was removing him from an abundantly fruitful mission in Samaria to no purpose. Acts 8:26 significantly elucidates that Philip was sent to a wilderness – "this is a desert road". God had his long term purposes for the continent of Africa, but Philip could not see the future. God seemed to have asked him to abandon sensible missionary strategy.

Although every human strategy must remain subject to the over-ruling guidance of God, submission to the Spirit does not normally require the abandonment of human reason or methodologies. We are merely required to exercise such flexible obedience that follows the Lord's directions even when we do not understand how they fit in with overall biblical patterns of strategy. The example of Philip further illustrates the fact that God's Spirit may not normally work directly without using human agencies. Although the Ethiopian eunuch had "come to Jerusalem to worship" and was also studying a wonderful Isaianic prophecy about the

Messiah, yet still the Spirit chose to use a human agent
to bring this man to faith in Jesus Christ.

As Christ's disciples we are called to be "God's fellow-
workers". The Holy Spirit uses us and our abilities in
his service. Dr. Tippett adds in *Church Growth and the
Word of God*: "the undeniably right idea of God's sovereignty and our obedience can be abused when man is
seen as a *mere instrument* in God's hand and not in any
way a *responsible agent*."

Realisation of this truth releases us from fear of using
natural human gifts in our ministries for the Lord. Some
Christians fear to develop skills in communication or
construct a strategy for the evolution of their church lest
they be guilty of being carnal. Fear of so-called "gimmicry" may stifle effective ministry.

If we believe that the Holy Spirit uses means, then we
shall also want to study what particular means he has
used in the course of the history of the Church. Christians will find it helpful to analyse the causes for the
growth or stagnation of the church in their own and in
other lands. Some such studies fall into the danger of
reading preconceived ideas into the facts of Church history, but nevertheless a careful study of Church history
may reveal to us patterns and principles for the work of
the Spirit. Such study should not only look at the history
of the Church in past centuries, but also at recent developments in a wide variety of countries.

We shall now therefore look at some causes of numerical growth in the Church which seem to be common
patterns for the working of the Holy Spirit.

2 FACTORS IN CHURCH LIFE

In the Old Testament Israel was called to live such a life of holiness that God's blessing would shine gloriously in her national life. This would attract the surrounding nations and draw them spontaneously to Jerusalem to worship the God of Israel. Isaiah prophesied of the hill upon which the temple was built: "all the nations shall flow to it, and many peoples shall come" (Isa. 2:2). He gloried in the prospect of the day when "his glory will be seen upon you" (Isa. 60:2) with the result that "nations shall come to your light, and kings to the brightness of your rising" (Isa. 60:3). "Nations that knew you not shall run to you" (Isa. 55:5) and "many peoples and strong nations shall come to seek the Lord of hosts in Jerusalem, and to entreat the favour of the Lord" (Zech. 8:22). Micah also shares in this same brilliant dream of that great day when "peoples shall flow to it, and many nations shall come and say: 'come, let us go up to the mountain of the Lord . . . that he may teach us his ways'" (Mic. 4:2).

The godly remnant of Israel reached out to attain this mirage, but the people's sinful and rebellious corruption turned this vision to ashes. With broken hearts the prophets repeatedly warned God's people that sin would bring inevitable judgment at the hands of the heathen nations which surrounded Israel. As a result the nations would hiss at them and despise both Israel and her God.

But the life-giving light of the world would come. The perfect Israelite would emerge from centuries in the wings and take his rightful place in the centre of the stage. He would attract representatives of the nations to himself and would prove to be the way to the Father. The wise men from the east would come to him to bring their gifts in fulfilment of Isa. 60:6 – "they shall bring gold and frankincense, and shall proclaim the praise of the Lord". The Canaanite woman with the demon-possessed daughter came with faith to him for healing, defying the discouraging words of Jesus, "I was sent only to the lost sheep of the house of Israel" (Matt. 15:24). One Roman centurion found healing for a slave "who was dear to him" (Luke 7:2) and was encouraged by Jesus' marvelling comment, "not even in Israel have I found such faith" (Luke 7:9); another centurion at the cross was jolted into an awe-filled confession: "truly this was the son of God!"

John's Gospel shows Jesus to be the fulfilment of the Old Testament, and the climax of this teaching is the coming of the Greeks spontaneously to Jesus in John 12. When Jesus hears that the Greeks want to see him, he responds with the excited statement that "the hour has come for the Son of man to be glorified" (John 12:23). Now he can move on to the supreme purpose of his life. His death and resurrection will lead to "much fruit", for he will draw "all men" to himself. His saving work as the light of the world means that life is available for "whoever believes" and "any one" who hears his sayings (John 12:24–47). With the fulfilment of the Old Testament in the coming of the Gentiles to Jesus the way is open for the cross and resurrection. Salvation would no longer be centred on the temple in Jerusalem and be primarily for Jews; now the Gospel can reach out to people of all nations.

Jesus is the light who draws the nations *in* to himself. His apostles are called to be lights that shine *out* into the world. But out-going evangelistic mission is built upon the Old Testament foundation of a communal life which draws and attracts men to the light. The Church will never reach out effectively unless men may "see your good works" (Matt. 5:16). It is significant therefore that Paul foresees a time when "all Israel" will be saved because they are provoked to jealousy by the Gentile Christian Church (Rom. 11:11–27). The challenge to live such lives as provoke men to longing jealousy should not be diminished by our uncertainty as to exactly what Paul meant by "all Israel".

In this chapter therefore we want to examine certain factors in the life of the Church which may play a part in attracting men and women to the Church and thus to the Lord himself. We long that our churches may not be stumbling blocks which prevent people from considering the claims of Jesus Christ. It is sometimes said that many, particularly in the United Kingdom, believe in God and are attracted to the person of Jesus, but the image of the Church is a barrier to faith. Pope Paul VI in his 1975 "Evangelii Nuntiandi" likewise regretted to hear people "claiming to love Christ but without the Church, to listen to Christ but not the Church, to belong to Christ but outside the Church". The Church, as well as its individual members, needs to reflect the attractiveness of the Saviour. The witness of the individual Christian is greatly enhanced if the non-Christian can also see the communal testimony of a living church.

1. *Fellowship*

The opening verses of John's first letter struck me in a
new way recently. I had heard many talks expounding
these verses to show that our witness must stem from
personal experience of the Lord. It is of course a vital
truth that we are to proclaim "that which we have seen
and heard". But I had never heard an exposition of the
aim or purpose of this proclamation. The verse continues: "that which we have seen and heard we proclaim
also to you, *so that you may have fellowship with us*".
Our life as Christians together is so beautifully loving
that our great desire for other people is that they too
may share in our fellowship. What a challenge to the life
of the Church or Christian Union! It should be noted
that John is not talking of a merely human fellowship.
He proceeds with the reminder that "our fellowship is
with the Father and with his Son Jesus Christ" (1 John
1:3). A happy sense of togetherness may be attained by
men of the same background sharing the same interests
– e.g. a football club or at the pub. But the fellowship of
the Christian Church is to be a community of unselfish
loving service amongst all kinds of people. True love is a
fruit of the Spirit (Gal. 5:22) and stems from God who is
himself love (1 John 4:8). A truly loving fellowship will
therefore not emerge merely as a result of cups of coffee
or meals together, although the sharing of meals
together may well have been a part of normal church
life in the New Testament. In Jewish life the Passover
meal was a family celebration; the New Testament celebration of the sacrificial death of the perfect Passover

lamb was likewise a family feast. Now however our brothers and sisters are essentially those who share with us adoption as children of God. The Church is our new family and we share this celebratory feast together as brothers and sisters in Christ. In Middle Eastern society the act of eating together is a meaningful sign of fellowship. It is sad that the Lord's Supper has often lost the joyful informality and togetherness of a shared meal.

But fellowship can not be forged by eating together. It is as we come together in open-hearted praise, prayer, confession and obedient listening to the voice of God in Scripture that true fellowship will be built. This will be further enhanced by obedient service of the Lord together in service to the world around us. I was encouraged to meet several people at St. Michael-le-Belfrey in York who were attracted to the church and then converted through the obvious joy in fellowship they saw there.

We live today in a lonely world. Family relationships are breaking down. Parents and children often find communication hard. Husbands and wives find their love together under constant attack. To many the home has ceased to be a haven of love and peace. Dr. Leslie Allen in his New International Commentary on Micah states that "man is so made that he finds security in a small group among whom he is accepted and receives support. At the heart of the concentric circles of people known to him there must ever be a stable core of friends, and usually family, if his psychological equilibrium is to be maintained." How horrible therefore is the picture of Micah 7:5,6 where "the son treats the father with contempt, the daughter rises up against her mother" and man can "put no trust in a neighbour, have no confidence in a friend". To those who suffer the consequences of such a breakdown of relationships in society the rich fellowship of the Church beckons attractively. In the lonely individualism of urban society the Christian yearns that his neighbour should "have fellowship with us". The Gospel is indeed "good news" and meets the heart-felt needs of modern man. This is true not only of western countries, but also wherever the shelter of tribal entities or of extended families is shattered by modern urbanisation. The Kenyan theologian John Mbiti is right to see the Church as the "new tribe".

Where the Church demonstrates such loving fellowship, people will be attracted and the Church will grow.

But the New Testament word "fellowship" seems to mean more than just richly loving relationship in Christ. It probably relates to the Old Testament word "justice" which is one of the basic characteristics of the Kingdom of God. In the Old Testament justice was not what Segundo (*The Liberation of Theology*) calls a "neutral, antiseptic term". Justice demanded concrete action within the covenant people of God. The Law was to be administered for the protection of the weak. Widows and orphans were to be cared for. Foreigners were not to be exploited, for Israel had experienced herself the agonies of slavery and exploitation in Egypt. In the New Testament we observe similar requirements within the fellowship of God's covenant people. James reveals that such groups as widows who lacked "muscle" were not to be neglected. And in fact the widows seem to have become a significant grouping within the church (e.g. Acts 9:39,41; 1 Tim, 5:3, 9–16).

Crime may not pay, but "muscle" certainly does. In most societies today the weak go to the wall. Paul however reminds the elders at Ephesus that they "must help the weak" (Acts 20:35) and he himself gave an example. To the Thessalonians also he writes that they should "help the weak" (1 Thess. 5:14). Such fellowship which lovingly supports the weak will surely prove a magnet to despised elements in society. Some people are deeply concerned at the large number of psychologically unstable Christians in the churches and Christian Unions of our country. Serious depression haunts the corridors even of our training colleges from which the future leadership of our churches will graduate. Of course the presence of such deep personal needs challenges the pastoral concern of Christian leaders at every level, but we rejoice that the Christian fellowship continues its historic role in providing shelter, comfort and love to people in need. Christ welcomes the weak and poor in spirit, the unloved child of a broken home, the man who cannot succeed in his work or who is a social misfit – the warmth of a loving Christian fellowship draws them towards the welcoming embrace of Christ. Leprosy patients all over the world – the faceless poor in Latin American shanty towns – lonely old ladies in European high-rise flats; in Christ God calls them "my people" and in the Church they are addressed as "brother" and "sister". No wonder the Church has always attracted the weaker elements of society! And thus the Church grows.

"That which we have seen and heard we proclaim also to you, so that you may have fellowship with us" (1 John 1:3).

2 *Miracles*

"Unless God steps in with a miracle or gives him a decisive vision, it seems that he will never become a Christian," said a new missionary to me in Singapore. She was referring to her Muslim language teacher. He had known and taught many new missionaries and through them had both seen and heard much concerning the Lord. He was impressed by the individual lives of his students and also by the atmosphere of the whole missionary school. He had read from the New Testament and come to see something of the beauty of Jesus. But he was not a strong personality. Courage and absolute conviction are essential before a man will turn from Islam to Christ.

I was reminded of my Muslim friend Aziz. He too had enjoyed close friendship with several of us over a period of some ten years. At first he was not interested in the Gospel, but gradually he became convinced of its truth. No, it was not just the truth of Christ which impressed him – he saw that the Gospel had unique power to change the whole character of his people. Aziz was deeply concerned for his fellow Malays. The Gospel could make them honest, industrious and more reliable. He expressed to us his desire that he and his whole people might become followers of Jesus Christ, but . . . "Do you want me to be killed?", Aziz asked me twice when I urged him to take the vital step of committing himself to Christ and decide to express his faith openly. Although he was a police sergeant in the thriving modern state of Singapore, he was right to face the very real risk. In a totally Muslim community apostasy often means death.

I knew the sad truth of this, for we had already experienced the death of three sisters who had expressed an interest in the Christian faith. We did not know whether they had actually put their faith in Christ, but the shame of possible apostacy from Islam had moved their mother to put poison in their tea and kill them.

It is relatively easy for Christians to face possible martyrdom when they have already known the glorious grace of the Lord in personal experience. Aziz and our language teacher were facing a more difficult choice. Before ever experiencing the love and salvation of Christ they already had to risk the possibility of a martyr's death.

Perhaps the new missionary was right. Without a miracle or some impressive vision such men would remain inwardly believing, but would never have the absolute assurance which would give them the courage to take an open stand as Christians. As far as I know, neither Aziz nor our language teacher has ever made a decisive committal to Christ.

"We must pray and ask the Lord to give them the miracle they need," said the new missionary. I saw the validity of her thinking, but I queried the rightness of such a prayer. The Bible is obviously full of stories of God's miracles. My own experience supported this, for I had seen God working marvellous miracles for me in my early days as a Christian in Britain and then also later when my wife and I worked as missionaries in Indonesia. Miraculous answers to prayer was one thing, but to expect God to give miracles to non-Christians with the specific purpose of convincing them of the vital truth of the Christian faith is quite another matter. I was forced to think again.

The evidence of the New Testament points to the

reality of miraculous signs accompanying the preaching of the word. Thus the Gospel was seen as well as heard. Michael Green in his *Evangelism in the Early Church* is surely right when he says of exorcisms that they were "clearly designed to back up the claims of the preached word" and that they "had a great converting effect in an age which was hag-ridden with the fear of demonic forces dominating every aspect of life and death". He further asserts that "perhaps the greatest single factor which appealed to the man in the street was deliverance, deliverance from demons, from fate, from magic". In similar vein he adds "the proclamation of Jesus as Lord indicated his sovereignty over the demons, and it made a very great appeal".

(a) *Exorcism* In many areas of the world today the powers of magic and demonic spirits bind men still in chilling fear. The saving word of the Gospel of a loving Jesus may entice frightened hearts, but the imprisoning power of evil spirits will prevent conversion to Christ. Failure to demonstrate the power of Christ leaves men still in the clutches of fear. A weak Jesus is no match for powerful demonic forces!

Roland Allen in *Missionary Methods: St. Paul's or ours?* likewise notes that "Jesus' miracles were a visible sign to the whole world of the nature and purpose of his teaching" and he sees the early Church's miracle-working power as "a most valuable weapon with which to confute opponents and to convince the hesitating" because it was a proof of Christ's "superior authority over all the heathen gods and demons". Yes, it is this power which the world needs to see!

Demonic powers show their reality and power in

every continent. Islam has always from its earliest in-
ception allowed animistic spirit powers to have a continued place in the Muslim religion. Although the
Quran castigates all forms of idolatry, the reality of evil
spirits and their activities is never negated by the power
of Allah. Throughout the Islamic world therefore we
still find occult powers and practices.

Hinduism and Buddhism together with other eastern
religions are very inclusive by nature. Syncretistic incorporation of elements of earlier faiths is assumed. (Although Buddhism is a reaction against Hinduism, it
nevertheless assumes many of the basic philosophical
ideas and religious values of the religion from whose
womb it was born. Eastern religions can prove fiercely
intolerant of anyone who is dogmatic in asserting
unique truth, but they are generally tolerant of any all-
embracing tolerance.) The power of occult spirits is a
vital part of daily life in such contexts.

In Latin America the enforced mass conversion of
the Indian peoples merely masked the continued existence of primal religious beliefs and forms with all the
attendant spirit forces. And in Brazil the slave population from West Africa further introduced the now
prevalent spiritism and voodoo.

Sophisticated Europe with centuries of Christian
heritage has never totally conquered the forces of magic
and occult spirits. With the decline of the Christian
Church over the past century these forces have come to
the fore. Near us at All Nations Christian College there
is a village with an active witches' coven which claims to
have its roots in pre-Christian British animism. For centuries it survived in extreme secrecy, but more recently

it has functioned quite openly. They have even put on a play about witchcraft in the local College of Further Education. New recruits have been added to their number. Spiritual hardness has characterised all Christian work in that village. The local churches find the going heavy. Youth work has produced damage to church property, but there has been little evidence of the life-giving work of the Spirit. Just in the last year or so specific prayer has however resulted in some definite conversions in the village. We have much to learn in the school of spiritual warfare. Contact with eastern religions, disillusionment with materialism and boredom with the humdrum of modern life have made people more susceptible. Young people in the schools experience the reality of moving glasses and the spirits of the ouija board; magic circles and séances abound – particularly in France where it is said that there are more mediums than Roman Catholic priests. In such circumstances fear grips the mind.

The Christian Church in recent years has tended either to ignore the miracle-working power of the Spirit of Christ or to use his power only within the context of the Christian fellowship. One church I know in Yorkshire has however openly ministered to people afflicted with demonic power and this has led to conversions. Likewise numerical growth came a few years ago to the youth work of a large church in the stockbroker belt south of London. The local grammar school had high hopes of university scholarships from a particularly bright group of sixth formers, but ouija sessions among these boys led to radical changes in their pattern of behaviour. Their work suffered and moral disorders began to run rife. The headmaster did not know how to handle the problem and asked the vicar to come to the school. Realising his own inexperience in occult questions, he asked his curate to deal with the situation as he had more personal experience. The curate was God's instrument in releasing the boys from the power of Satan with the result that many of them were converted and added to the Church. This influx of new life into the youth work made other young people reconsider the claims of Christ and so there were then yet other conversions. Such direct confrontation with satanic powers demonstrates the power and reality of the Lord in an age when many find it difficult to believe in a God who is personally involved in our daily lives.

Many Christians have underplayed the element of the miraculous in the Christian faith because it has sometimes been associated with religious extremism or with doctrinal positions which they may reject. But misuse of God's gifts should in no way turn us from a right and proper use. Thus some in the early Church misused the doctrine of justification by faith and made it an excuse for riotous licence (cf. Rom. 6:1), but Paul did not therefore renounce the true doctrine. There are religious fanatics who misuse the reality of Christ's power. To some the use of the miraculous is associated with particular doctrinal views on the baptism of the Spirit. But whatever our theological beliefs on this latter subject, all of us must surely agree that in the Scriptures our God has power to work miracles. We are all surely agreed that God's power is the same today. Let us expect him to work in power!

Even where Christians have acknowledged God's

power in exorcism we have tended to expect him to work only for Christians within the context of the Church. Believers with former occult connections find release in the name of Jesus Christ. But few of us have followed the early apologists who, according to Roland Allen, appealed to the Lord's power over demons "as a signal proof of the superiority of Christianity over heathen religions". People need to hear and see that the power of Jesus Christ is greater than all demonic powers. They can therefore turn to the Lord without undue fear and with confidence that he will prove a strong fortress to protect and liberate them.

(b) *Healing* But exorcism is not the only form of miracles! Healing miracles may equally attract people to the love of Christ. In countries where medical facilities are few or where poverty prevents people using these facilities, there God seems to pour out this particular gift of healing in abundance. D'Epinay in his fascinating survey on the Pentecostals of Chile (*Haven of the Masses*) points out that the commonest spiritual gift among Pentecostal pastors in Chile is the gift of healing, not the gift of tongues. In Britain the gift of tongues is for many a clear evidence of the reality of God's Spirit at work; to British Pentecostals it has been taken as *the* proof of being filled with the Spirit. In much of Latin America however the gift of healing is more vitally relevant to peoples' needs and therefore takes precedence. In the poverty of the sprawling shantytowns around the mushrooming cities the miracle of physical healing becomes precious and attractive.

Some people in these drab fringes of the cities may need to save for months before they can afford to visit a doctor. Further extensive saving may follow before they can translate his prescription into healing drugs. Such prolonged delay could mean death or at least acute suffering. The vividly bright notices outside a Pentecostal church cannot but catch the invalid's attention: "Jesus Christ saves and heals" or "Healing Service on Wednesday at 7 p.m. – preacher Brother N".

His motive for attending the service may be more for physical healing than for salvation from sin, but God can meet men at their particular point of need before leading them on to a fuller appreciation of all he gives us in Christ. In the New Testament too, many came to Jesus for healing, but went away with sins forgiven.

Having found healing in the mid-week meeting, a man will also come to appreciate the sense of personal worth which he will now have in the fellowship of the church. In the shantytown he is a nobody, but in the church he is called "brother" and can participate in prayer and testimony in all the meetings. He has a new worth as he becomes part of this vibrant new family. His healing therefore is not just physical, but also social and psychological as well as spiritual.

Pastoral counsellers today talk much of man's need of "worth" and "acceptance". But sadly our current society is causing many to grow up without this precious assurance. Many therefore doubt whether God could truly be interested in them and even love them. How reassuring it is for such people when God graciously heals them of some sickness or performs some other definite miracle for them in direct answer to prayer! In Christ a man is accepted and loved; he *does* have worth in the eyes of God. And like his Latin American equivalent he then also finds that same new sense of worth when he is accepted as a valued brother by the Christian community. He has a new family where he can love and be loved.

The healing ministry is not restricted to poorer countries where sickness abounds without financial resources for effective medical treatment. Even in advanced technological societies doctors are not omniscient or all-powerful. Solutions to various diseases elude them. As one virus is conquered, another springs up to baffle us. Here too miraculous healing in answer to direct prayer plays a growing part in the life and ministry of the Christian Church. In recent years in Britain the healing ministry has come into new prominence in many churches. Controversy has raged medically about these miracles, but meanwhile some people have turned to Christ because of such visible manifestations of his power. Many British ministers and lay Christians are venturing into this area of ministry almost against their will and with very wavering faith at first.

God may use people in his healing work who would not normally claim to have a gift of healing. This was my own experience. I was in East Malaysia doing Bible teaching in various up-country churches. While I was visiting one particular village, a young couple from another racial group arrived with a small child who was obviously desperately ill. They had no language in common with the rest of us there, but they used signs to tell us they knew we were Christians and they asked us to pray. Their signs showed simple faith that a Christian's prayer would surely result in healing.

As the visiting speaker I was asked to pray for the

child. It was embarrassing; everyone else seemed confident in faith while the much trumpeted Bible teacher from overseas lacked the faith to believe that healing would follow from his prayer! I had no option – my hand was forced. With faltering faith I prayed. The child was healed. God does work.

Healing meets more than merely physical needs. Psychological disturbances increasingly invade our society. A fast changing world and the tragic breakdown of family life have contributed to the growth of insecurity. The powerful touch of the miracle-working Christ can bring a new sense of peace within as we come to rest in the sure knowledge of his love and grace towards us. The security of knowing that we are loved can give us a new sense of worth and wholeness. Peace may issue from the assurance of all sin and guilt having been utterly paid for and therefore removed through the atoning and redemptive work of Jesus on the Cross.

God answers prayer and desires to heal us in every area of our being. He wants us to be whole, for this is the full meaning of "salvation". Sometimes he will work through doctors, pastoral counsellors and psychiatrists. At other times he will work more directly through evident miracles. In either case it is His Name which should be glorified. And as people see that he is a God who loves his people, answers their prayers and has the power and will to heal, they will be drawn in response to him.

(c) *Visions* God may also attract men to himself through the experience of a vision or dream. In biblical times God clearly spoke through this means. Modern psychology since the days of Jung has made westerners exceedingly suspicious of this phenomenon. As with all spiritual gifts there is need of discernment where the content of the vision is submitted to the test of Scripture. But God will speak to Christian and non-Christian alike through such means.

When touring East Malaysia for Bible teaching I was told of a striking example of a vision. A Muslim soldier was enduring guard duty in the solitary midnight hours when suddenly the sky lit up with a brilliant pure light in the shape of a cross. He knew that this was the emblem of Christians, but assumed that it had no significance for him as a Muslim. He therefore woke up two Christian soldiers from his barracks and together they stood in the open air staring up at the cross. The Christians explained to their friend the glories of the Cross of Christ, relating its splendour to the purity of the vision above them. They assured him that the cross had been purposely revealed to him, for the Lord desired his salvation. So the vision and the clear, relevant words of the Christian soldiers combined to bring this man to faith in Jesus Christ.

Recently a student in Bristol was led to faith through hearing an audible voice from heaven. Another student there was delivered from an occult background when a vivid vision of the Cross of Christ moved her to call out to the Lord. A friend of mine from a totally irreligious background was working on the factory floor when he heard a voice. He knew immediately that God was speaking and he fell on his knees beside his lathe and gave his life to the Lord.

The miracle-working power of the Spirit of the Lord can prove a vital force to quicken the growth of the

Church. The caveat must however be sounded that this may lead to frothy sensationalism unless the signs are accompanied by a preaching of the whole counsel of God and followed by careful teaching of the converts. Many Pentecostal churches in Latin America have suffered the consequence of failure in meaty biblical preaching and teaching. Miracles can draw multitudes to the Church, but such converts may prove shallow and fickle if left untaught. Jesus himself saw such crowds evaporate when subjected to the challenging demands of his spoken word. How much we all need to learn to love the Giver, not merely his gifts!

3 *Morals*

As we read the Epistles we are shocked to observe the apparently low moral standards which could remain even in churches which knew the glories of the Gospel. Women quarrelled in the Philippian church (Phil. 4:2); laziness and gossip characterised the busybodies in Thessalonica, and Timothy's companions (2 Thess. 3:11 and 1 Tim. 5:13); immorality assailed the churches of Pergamum and Thyatira (Rev. 2:14, 20). And moral sins of various sorts characterised the Corinthian church – divisive party-spirit, sexual disorders, selfish greed at the Lord's Supper, the folly of going to law against one another.

Our admiration for the New Testament churches and our ambition to be like them need to be qualified by a realisation that the first century believers were as human as ourselves!

Could God really use such instruments in his holy service?

(a) *Gradual growth* Many of us who go overseas to serve in the younger churches can be thrilled by their lively enthusiasm, but at the same time shocked by their spiritual poverty and the low level of sanctification.

Our biblical picture of conversion is new birth. Through faith in the crucified and risen Christ we are born again to a new life. The imagery of new birth assumes that we begin as weak, little babes in the Christian life and then gradually grow. As I have expounded elsewhere (see the author's *Don't Just Stand There*), one characteristic in the New Testament teaching of the Kingdom of God is precisely this point – the Kingdom starts small and then grows gradually, like a seed becoming a tree, or leaven spreading through the whole loaf. Jesus himself, the king of the kingdom, came as a baby and then "increased in wisdom and in stature, and in favour with God and man" (Luke 2:52). The Jews had expected the Kingdom to come suddenly in a flash of time: they expected it to come in perfection. Jesus' teaching concerning the gradual growth of the Kingdom introduced a totally new element into theological thought. The sudden perfect coming of the Kingdom awaits us at the second coming of Jesus when his reign shall be perfect. Meanwhile gradual growth characterises the Christian life in us as individuals and in the Church as a whole.

Small beginnings contain the potential for greater developments. Newly converted believers and recently established churches have just begun the long upward path of becoming increasingly like their Lord. At the outset of new life in Christ many facets of the old life still remain entrenched. The rocket is still in the world's atmosphere, but the potential is there for the climb into more rarefied heavenly heights!

We must not force young Christians to moral standards beyond their spiritual years. We long for sanctification because we know this to be God's will (1 Thess. 4:3), but we must allow the Holy Spirit to lead people forward at his own pace. We can teach and expound the Scriptures, showing the perfect standards of holiness which God enjoys. But we must not enforce moral laws too early, thus introducing a legalistic approach. Enforced legalistic sanctification which does not touch the heart will lead to hypocrisy. Such legalism may be introduced through social pressure or by means of specific church rules, but in either case it will damage the Spirit-led development of the Christian and it will hamper the growth of the Church.

The world outside the Church quickly observes the difference between genuine sanctification and enforced ethical standards. The former attracts men to Christ; the latter may repel and thus also prevent the numerical growth of the Church. So both the quantitative and the qualitative growth of the Church is impeded.

(b) *Culture and ethics* Church growth may further be hindered by unbiblical cultural approaches to ethics. The imposition of moral values which are irrelevant to current situations makes the Church appear outdated and irrelevant. Such imposition may result from a hangover of moral concepts from a previous generation or it may come from foreign sources.

When I first began to follow Christ seriously it was assumed among live Christians that taboos on dancing, cinema attendance, alcoholic beverages, etc., were a necessary element in discipleship. Even the most scrupulous examination of the Bible could hardly find biblical evidence for such prohibitions as *necessary*. In certain cultural situations particular non-biblical practices may prove expedient, but we must be careful not to make them into rigid rules or continue them beyond their time. As social situations change, so the ethical guide-lines of the Church may need to be altered in conformity with the needs of the day. This does not mean a mere "situational ethic", for some commandments are clear and specific in Scripture. These do not change. Biblical principles also remain, but their application will alter with the changes in society. If the Church becomes out-dated in these matters it will become stagnant. On the other hand, ethical relevance which really speaks to the current needs of society will make a deep impression and attract men to the Gospel of Christ.

Despite our best intentions not to impose foreign concepts, missionaries have always faced the danger of bringing the ethical outlook of their home countries. We have introduced our own ideas on the relative "badness" of particular sins, whereas all of us have at some stage been shocked by Paul's lists of works of the flesh in which he juxtaposes such sins as jealousy and envy with sorcery and idolatry (Gal. 5:19ff); or in 2 Tim. 3:2 the fearful list of adjectives "proud, arrogant, abusive . . . inhuman, implacable . . . profligates" brackets what might to us be a lesser and more everyday sin "disobedient to their parents". Roman Catholic theology may distinguish between moral and venial sins; Islam too lists the seventeen "Kabirah" (major sins) as opposed to the innumerable forms of "Saghirah" (lesser sins). God however hates all sins equally.

The Karo Batak people, with whom my wife and I worked in Indonesia, have different feelings from ourselves with regard to moral issues. Underhand sins like gossip or sly pick-pocketing were considered gross evils, while the more open forms of sin like hitting someone on the nose were relatively minor. This clearly affected attitudes to Church teaching and discipline.

One of the largest Indonesian Churches was split into two factions, each owing allegiance to different millionaires. One Sunday a large city congregation found two ministers in their midst, each trying to enter the pulpit to take the service and preach. A fight developed. The police were called, batons were wielded, one minister was removed and the other propelled into the pulpit. He preached an evangelistic sermon and several were born again of the Spirit of God that morning. I questioned the providence of God in allowing his Spirit to work in such a situation through such an apparently unclean channel. An Indonesian friend tactfully pointed out that some European ministers through gossip undercut the reputation of other Christians, but still God sometimes uses them to bring salvation to their people. For me it was an encouraging reminder that in his grace God may even use imperfect agents like us.

To us a fight in a church is such a scandal that it would prevent outsiders being attracted to Christ, but we must not impose our scale of sins' relative seriousness upon other peoples. If we do, we make the Gospel sadly unattractive and hinder therefore the growth of the Church.

This applies equally to the imposition of taboos from a past cultural situation which can make the Christian faith look antiquated. My wife has occasionally been criticised for wearing trouser suits because the Bible opposes transvestite perversion! To her elderly critics only men wear trousers! Likewise outdated attitudes to the length of men's hair may make a Christian look an oddity unnecessarily. On one occasion when speaking at a University Christian Union I noticed one young man with neatly cut short hair when all the other students had much longer hair. He came from a somewhat narrow Christian background and I was not surprised to discover from him that he was having real problems relating to life at university – his hair betrayed his problem!

For healthy growth a church should include within its membership believers at every stage of Christian maturity. There should be some older, more mature Christians whose lives testify to God's holiness and demonstrate the sanctifying grace of the Lord. They are a living proof that growth in Christ is a reality. But there should also be new believers recently added to the church; their new-found faith with the lively enthusiasm of fresh love will relate more easily to their friends, neighbours and workmates who will see that Jesus Christ saves and changes men like themselves.

4 *Doctrine*

Hackles rise and defensiveness bristles at the very mention of doctrine! But churches can only grow as the message of grace in Jesus Christ is effectively preached. Christians will only develop and mature in faith as the truths of Christ grip their hearts. We must therefore face the issue of doctrine if we are to examine what encourages or hinders the growth of God's Church.

(a) *Irrelevant quarrels* In former times Jewish scholars debated whether God worked on the Sabbath. Some said that he was too holy to break his own Law, while others asserted that the universe depends for its continued existence on the continual providence of God. Jesus stepped into the heart of this debate by healing a man on the Sabbath and then stating categorically, "my Father is working still, and I am working" (John 5:17). The tenses of the verbs denote the continuous non-stop working of God and of his son, Jesus.

Christian scholars can equally alienate the ordinary man in the street with similar ivory-tower arguments. At one time Christian theologians worried over how many angels could dance on the point of a pin. Are we still today in danger of fiddling while the world around us burns? What impression does the outsider have when he hears our heated arguments about insignificant details?

As a missionary one has to adjust to the religious debates of various nations. In the U.S.A., for example, the searchlight is frequently focused on particular views concerning the second coming of Christ; many will consider a pre-millennial viewpoint essential doctrine.

In western countries some denominational divisions are based on baptism. Immersion or sprinkling? Infant or believers' baptism? A leading Nigerian pastor listened to some British students debating these questions. Noting his silence they eventually asked him what was done about baptism in his church in Nigeria. His reply left them baffled, "Oh, we're just biblical," he said, "we practise both infant and believers' baptism, using immersion or sprinkling according to the desire of the persons concerned." He was unconvinced that the Bible gave clear prescriptions concerning the mode or timing of baptism. He was however firm on the covenantal significance of baptism theologically.

Let us not be side-tracked by such quarrels and divisions!

(b) *Outmoded thought forms* The average Christian is very weak indeed in his understanding of the doctrine of the Trinity. The old Greek philosophical background to the basic words used in our trinitarian formulations is quite meaningless to most of us – "person", "nature", "substance", etc. The Church fathers were right to use the thought forms and language of pagan Greek to define their faith in a way that was meaningful to them and to their generation. The New Testament Church did very similarly in translating the message of Christ into the language and thought forms of the contemporary Gentile world as well as in relating the Messiah to their Jewish compatriots.

We need to restate the unchanging message of the Gospel with relevant terminology so that we may "make it clear as we ought to speak" (Col. 4:4). The original Hebrew concepts were brilliantly translated into Greek; later, as R. Boyd pointedly shows in *The Latin Captivity of the Church*, the Greek was manhandled into Latin with considerable loss en route. Today the Latin justification, redemption, propitiation, etc., require retranslation into modern English.

In the past a high proportion of our population attended biblically orientated religious education classes at school or even went to Sunday school. Problems of communication were therefore relatively trivial. But today a new generation has emerged which no longer understands the old religious language of the church.

This struck me afresh when I was returning from missionary service in Indonesia. Our ship sailed through the Suez Canal and we enjoyed the splendid beauty of a setting sun on the mountains of the Sinai range. I joined the crowds of Australians along the rails of the deck as we all drank in the view. I wondered how to share Christ with them.

"Strange to think of old Moses being given the Law up on these mountains," I said to my neighbours. Not one of them had ever heard of Moses. I asked them if they had not seen the film of the Ten Commandments. Several had seen it but it had not occurred to them that it related a historical or biblical event; to them it had been just another fictional film.

It is hard for all the professions to make their language understandable to the man in the street. Doctors, scientists and engineers often baffle their hearers with technical terms. Christians do the same. It is our job, however, to make our message "clear, as we ought to speak" (Col. 4:4).

What we say is less important than what people hear. As Christians we cannot agree with Goethe when he said that words are given to man to conceal his thoughts. We want to communicate.

Our message needs to be related to the religious and philosophical thought forms of the people amongst whom we are working. The facts of biblical truth must not be compromised or relativised, but they must be made intelligible in the context of different systems of thought. Otherwise we shall fail to relate to the particular religious assumptions which underlie peoples' thought.

The contextualization of theological and biblical thought has become a major issue these days. Latin Americans are trying to look anew at Scripture and theology to see what they have to say about the Christian in a society of oppression and gross injustice. The Africans want answers to problems with regard to their relationship with their ancestors and with the surrounding natural order. They also look back in search of the African soul and question what is the relationship of the Christian faith to African primal religion. Indians have for many years been grappling with the attempt to express the Christian faith in terms intelligible to Hindu philosophy and beliefs. Thus the great Indian theologian Brahmabandhab Upadhyaya tries to relate to the monist stream of Hindu thought, in which there is no reality except Brahman – all is Brahman who cannot be described by any such finite descriptions as "personal". Further east in Taiwan the Chinese theologian Choan Seng Song has been looking at the relationship between the biblical "Shalom" and the Taoist concept of harmony in the Tao. He has also been concerned to relate the Confucian emphasis on pragmatic ethical issues to the more traditional Christian emphasis on the person and work of Christ, thus majoring on the doctrine of Christology. The Japanese Kitamori wrestled with suffering, for this was central to the post-war Japanese atmosphere. With supreme emphasis on the Cross he described suffering as in itself redemptive. This however led him to a grave weakness in respect to the Resurrection. His disciple Koyama was a missionary to Buddhist Thailand and sought to define the nature of God in such a way that would not be emprisoned by the impassive nature of the Buddha. He therefore emphasised the wrath of God to underline the fact that God is a free agent in his dealings with the world and is not to be "domesticated".

Such men are attempting to relate the Christian truth to their own particular situations in order that the Gospel may not appear to be what Roland Allen called "an exotic". They run into dangers. In such restatements of the Christian faith there is always an element of risk that we fall into syncretism or universalism. But nevertheless they challenge us to make our Gospel applicable to every cultural, religious and philosophical background. The pressing necessity of re-thinking our faith applies not only to missionaries overseas, but also to western churches in modern multi-racial society.

I was excited to meet a student worker at the Indian University of Westville in South Africa. He was using the thought of Keshab Chandra Sen (who also influenced Brahmabandhab Upadhyaya in the same direction) to describe the reality of the triune God in the traditional Hindu philosophical terms of Saccidananda. He related *Sat*/ultimate Truth to the Father as Creator; *Cit*/Intelligence, wisdom and good which move in relationship to man was related to Jesus Christ who is the Wisdom and who moves towards man in his incarnation; *Ananda*/joyful bliss and beautiful purity naturally relates to the Holy Spirit.

Philosophical climates also change from generation

to generation in every society. The expression of an unchanging Christian Gospel must therefore be related to
the vocabulary and philosophy of the people. In Britain,
as in other countries, thought forms and use of words
change rapidly these days and the Church is compelled
to face this or stagnate. How far can we use the terminology of the drug culture, for example, and then infuse
genuine Christian content by good teaching? Can the
Christian "pilgrimage" or "walk" be expressed as a
"trip with Jesus"? The dangers of this may frighten us –
but did the early Christians blanch at the use of Greek
terms to express great biblical realities? Mission in
today's changed and changing cultural milieu faces the
same fundamental problems of communication as the
early Church or any missionary situation.

If we fail to express the wonderful truths of the
Christian faith in relevant and intelligible modern dress,
then non-Christians will not be drawn to the Lord because they cannot truly understand the content of our
preaching. Likewise Christians will find it hard to ap-
propriate biblical doctrine and thus grow in understanding and love of the Lord. We shall also risk serious
inroads from heretical sects who will naturally exploit
those areas of truth which we fail to relate relevantly.

(c) *Unrelated witness* The Gospel needs not only to be
restated in current language and philosophical thought
forms, but it must also relate to the beliefs and questions
of the recipient.

Some years ago I visited a very lively parish church
which happened to contain within its parish boundaries
a sprinkling of Pakistani Muslims. It was encouraging
and personally challenging to observe the Christians'

determination to witness to their Muslim neighbours. I was told that they had recently visited every Muslim home to present a copy of Mark's Gospel to each household.

How sad to see such lively witness vitiated by ignorance! Mark's Gospel is of course the last Gospel to give to a Muslim. The very first verse will so anger him that he will not read any further. The great stumbling block to Christian witness to Muslims is our belief in Jesus as the Son of God. We should not alienate the Muslim by using this name for the Lord in our very first contact with him. Let us begin our witness more peaceably! At some later stage in his enquiry concerning Jesus we shall have to confront him with the fundamental disagreements between our two faiths, but let him first be introduced to the beauty of the person of Jesus in a less confrontational manner. Luke's Gospel is better related to Islamic ideas and so would seem to be the best introduction to Jesus for a Muslim.

Jesus did not present himself as God in the early stages of his disciples' relationship to him. Even the unpalatable truth of the Cross only became a central part of his teaching to them after they had begun to know him better and appreciate who he was. Jesus did not distort truth or trim his message to make it palatable; compromise ill befits him who is the truth. But Jesus did graciously lead his disciples gradually into all truth; they were not able at that stage to receive all that he had to tell them (John 16:12, 13). One step at a time the Lord led them. To baffle a small child with calculus before he has grasped basic arithmetic is not faithfulness to truth; it is folly and unkindness. To present the world with spiritual food which it cannot stomach can only cause the hardening experience of rejecting the Gospel.

(d) *What can we compromise?* Some members of the Church Growth movement have rightly pointed out that certain types of Christianity may be more acceptable in particular situations.

Dr. McGavran would stress that "the growth of the Church is the number one task of mission" and it could therefore be inferred that we must trim our doctrinal sails to the prevailing winds. If a particular theological approach prevents or hinders the achievement of this "number one task", should we abandon our cherished theologies?

Where do wisdom and cultural flexibility become downright compromise? None of us would consider it right to compromise on the fundamentals of clear biblical revelation.

As Dr. David Wells says in the closing summary of his *The Search for Salvation*: "The task is not so much that of finding new truths in the Bible, but of finding new ways of making it truth *for our world*." But we must not so adapt to what Karl Barth calls the moods, the modes of thought, the instincts, the ideas, the needs and aspirations of the world that our message is contaminated (*Church Dogmatics* iv, 3, 6).

Most of us would feel free to be tolerant and flexible with regard to minor peripherals which are not clearly spelled out in Scripture. Thus the doctrine of the atoning work of Christ and the fact of his resurrection or second coming are sacrosanct to us, even if such truths prove unpopular and their proclamation turns people away. Details of Church government might to some of us appear less central to our faith and less clear in the Bible; we might therefore feel free to adapt these to the cultural situation in which we happened to be placed. Our difficulty, however, is to determine where the line should be drawn between "fundamentals" and "peripherals".

We all want to remain faithful to God's biblical revelation. Such faithfulness holds higher priority than the pragmatic desire to see God's Church grow. Jesus himself did not compromise in declaring unpalatable truths even if they resulted in people rejecting him. So in Luke 4 he seemed to have won the admiration of the people of Nazareth (Luke 4:22), but then he alienated their sympathies by declaring that Gentiles receive God's grace in a way that Israel was unwilling to (Luke 4:24–27). This hard truth led them to be "filled with wrath" (Luke 4:28) and with murderous intention they rejected him (Luke 4:29).

We must therefore be faithful to revealed truth. But how does that relate to a humble awareness that other biblically based Christians hold different views on certain issues? Should we hold lightly to our understanding of Scripture if godly biblical scholars disagree on a particular point?

The balance between dogmatism and compromise is a tightrope. Mere pragmatic ends must not be the determining factor in deciding which theological means we use in mission.

3 FACTORS IN CHURCH STRUCTURES

We have already seen in the first chapter that the structural organisation of the Church needs to grow parallel to its numerical growth. It is also true that patterns of organisation will in their turn influence the growth or stagnation of the Church.

Calvin in the *Institutes of the Christian Religion* assumes that the Bible gives a blue-print concerning the organisation of the Church and its ministry. Thus in the context of his discussions on the eldership ("composed of pious, grave and venerable men"!), he states that "this arrangement was not confined to one age, and therefore we are to regard the office of government as necessary for all ages" (Book 4, Chapter 3, Section 8).

Anglican teaching on the other hand has always rejected the idea of a definite blueprint for Church government, but has rather allowed any system which is "consonant with Scripture".

One clear fact is that the New Testament Church emerged from its Jewish background with its church structures and worship patterns built on that foundation. Some theologians would seem to show that churches emerging among Gentiles followed the different organisational pattern of their particular backgrounds. From this we may argue that, with certain safeguards regarding basic biblical principles of Christian leadership, it would be right for churches to base their worship and structure on the cultural milieu in which they are located. Unsuitable structures and forms can inhibit the growth and life of a church.

1 *The Laity*

The leader of a European missionary society working in Japan sat in my study with an expression of distress clearly outlined on his face. "Japan is a land of problems," he informed me. "Most of our churches seem sound and healthy in every way, but for some reason they are stagnant and the Christians never quite seem to become effective workers. There are just a few churches which grow abundantly and whose members are vitally active for the Lord; but the ministers of those churches have become little dictators and we have failed to help them to become less autocratic."

Most missionaries come from lands which strongly emphasise the virtues of democracy and deplore dictatorships. The U.S.A., which supplies some 70 per cent of the total Protestant missionary force, has developed its whole national character on the foundation of strongly democratic values. The countries of western Europe have suffered the agonies of recent world wars because of evil dictatorships. We know the danger of absolute power corrupting absolutely – and Christians are not immune from the dangers of pride.

"Could it be that spiritually minded autocratic ministry suits Japan well?" I asked my friend. He was shocked at the very idea, but agreed that Japanese traditional society is far from democratic in character. Political, industrial and social structures all form pyramids under powerful leaderships. Together we discussed whether Japanese laity feel freer if they have to respond to strong authority than if they have to make their own decisions. A strong minister will see the gifts in his various church members and instruct them what role they are to play in the life and witness of the church. Group or committee leadership may leave the members bewildered, for they long to hear a word of authority which instructs with assurance. An autocratic leadership may result in the mobilisation of the laity.

In many western countries this was also the case a couple of decades ago. The strong one-man ministry with obvious preaching and teaching gifts was deeply appreciated. The laity responded to such leadership and became actively involved for the Lord. Today western society has changed. We have therefore reacted against the autocratic style of leadership where the minister holds all the reins in his hands.

Christians have come with renewed awareness to the biblical teaching of the Church as the body of Christ. Every member of that body has gifts and it is now realised that it is folly to expect the minister to be good at everything – pastoral counselling, preaching, administration, Bible teaching, childrens' work, etc. So the church has been struggling to evolve new structures which reflect the new situation. Should we have boards of elders with the minister as presiding elder? Should the minister be merely "primus inter pares" or should he retain ultimate authority and responsibility in his solitary hands? More adventurous churches have tried various experiments. Sometimes they have encountered grave teething problems and this can discourage some from making further progress in adjusting the structures of their church to the prevailing culture.

But culture never stands still. Many today question the viability of democracy, although they may still fear dictatorship. A strong lead does have some advantage. In some Christian circles too there is a new desire for the security of submitting to an authoritative leadership. The concept of the body is therefore reinterpreted. In Roman Catholic circles the expression "body" has been used traditionally to imply that which is under the direction of a head and neck. The Church as the body of Christ implies the supreme power of the hierarchy. Renewed emphasis in the Catholic Church on the role of the laity is expressed by the use of the term "the people of God". Among some Protestants too the expression "body" is coming to signify a group of mutually dependent Christians in intimate fellowship under authoritative leadership. Such discipleship groups can demonstrate the fellowship of the Christian faith in remarkable fashion with all the advantages of deep sharing in community, but they run the risk of extremes in the area of authority.

Depending on the cultural climate, both autocratic and democratic leadership structures can result in the mobilisation of the laity.

The Reformation has given Protestantism a rich heritage in the rediscovery of the doctrine of the priesthood of all believers. The Church is not just the hierarchy – it is the totality of the people of God. We cannot accept more traditional Catholic views in which the laity are "a mere accident, an appendix to the Church, necessary only to its bene esse" (Yves Congar in *Lay People in the*

Church). We rejoice to see in many areas of the Catholic Church also an emphasis on the laity. As far back as 1947 Pope Pius XII in his encyclical on the Liturgy *Mediator Dei* affirmed that the laity have a "priestly function" to fulfil. Hans Küng in *The Church* reminds us that "the laity is the Church, and the clergy its servants". Cardinal Suenens at a recent Synod of Bishops stressed the New Testament origin of the Church in a variety of independent local churches, while another cardinal said that "the pyramid structure of the Church will gradually disappear ... decision making will be more in the hands of local priests and laity."

The structures of the Church need to reflect our belief in the priesthood of all believers and the reality of the fact that "the laity is the Church" and not just "an appendix". This will facilitate growth, for if the Church is to grow healthily, the laity must play a decisive role.

(a) *The Laity in witness* It would seem that evangelism was not restricted in the early Church to the leaders of the Church, the apostles and elders. Although the Book of Acts largely confines itself to the missionary outreach of the apostles, it does also suggest that the outreach of the Church was on a larger scale than that. Thus in Acts 8:1 we read that "a great persecution arose against the church in Jerusalem; and they were all scattered ... except the apostles." We then find that in 8:4 "those who were scattered went about preaching the word". In writing to the Thessalonian Christians Paul is deeply thankful that the word of the Lord had "sounded forth from you in Macedonia and Achaia". Apparently the Christians must have travelled round these provinces proclaiming the message of Christ. The disciples must have learned their lesson early: "The harvest is plentiful" (Luke 10:2). It is impossible for a tiny handful of apostolic messengers to evangelise the multitudes of whole provinces and countries. The Lord therefore taught them to "Pray the Lord of the harvest to send out labourers into his harvest" (Luke 10:2). The urgency of such prayer will be matched by a continual emphasis in our ministry on the mobilisation of the laity for evangelistic witness. The British Church today is becoming increasingly aware of its minority position in the midst of a largely non-Christian population. We therefore struggle with the question of how we can inspire our laity to active mission.

There is a growing awareness today that laity are in closer contact than clergy or other full-time workers with the grass-roots of everyday life and ordinary people. They should have natural relationships and friendships with their neighbours and work colleagues. This allows them not only to share the Gospel by word, but also to support their verbal testimony with the realities of their everyday life and work. It also gives scope for a more gentle and gradual witness which does not force the message of Christ down peoples' throats in unpalatably large doses. Questions can be answered one at a time until the person is finally ready for commitment to Christ. The Christian in the world will have to face the problem of society and show that his Christian faith has significance within the situations which ordinary people face. The full-time Christian worker stands outside the problems and challenges of these economic and socio-political questions, but he will have to guide and teach his laity in such a manner that they are equipped to relate their biblical faith to such issues. It is the laity themselves who ultimately give witness to the world and in the world as to whether the Christian Gospel is in practice "good news" for every area of life. The laity are the Church's contact point with the outside world.

We should perhaps note at this stage that this applies to laity in their own country, but may be less true of those working in other lands. Expatriates are normally only invited to serve in specialised and highly-paid jobs for which nationals are still inadequately trained. This places the expatriate worker in an elitist position. Birds of a feather flock together, so he cannot expect close contact with local birds of poorer plumage. This may be more pronounced still if he is working in an area where only the highly educated speak adequate English. But among these leaders of society his influence may be felt.

In the west too we have encouraged the laity to play a vital part in the expansion of the Church through personal witness, bringing new people to the already existing Church. There is a need for every believer to be able to share his faith with his friends and lead them to personal faith in Jesus Christ. Sadly it remains true that many are quite unable to explain the Gospel in simple and concise terms; and if someone does prove to be open to the message of Christ, we may be unable to lead them acceptably to the life-changing decision of accepting Jesus as their Lord and Saviour.

Failure to prepare our Christians adequately for the ministry of personal evangelism has led to this vacuum being filled by unduly rigid and simplistic systems. It is biblically unjustifiable to insist on the same questions in the same strict order every time we witness. All men are different. Each has his own personality, his own problems and his own needs. We dare not ride rough-shod over individual personalities, submitting all sorts of people to identical witness techniques.

Such rigid systems may however be helpful for the beginner who may feel fearful of opening his mouth in evangelistic witness, but we must train and teach young Christians to outgrow them. Driving instructors give rigid rules for learners on how to start the car and pull out from the kerb. The more advanced driver follows the basic principles, but should not be tied within quite such a strait-jacket.

The emphasis on personal evangelism in the west has generally excluded any ambition to plant new churches. Such failure has been exacerbated by the rigidity of parish boundaries. In many of the Latin American Pentecostal churches baptismal preparation includes teaching on the need for church planting. Thus new Christians start their Christian life with this aim. As a result new Pentecostal churches spring up in many areas. While other churches are seeking to gather new people into their already existing congregations, the Pentecostals are free to establish new congregations in new population centres. The founding of new churches in Nigeria through the "New Life for All" movement was also largely the work of the laity. The multiplication of churches in Korea and Indonesia reflects the same truth. One church I know in Cheshire has also spawned other daughter churches through lay Christians. They have done this in various ways. One church was planted through placing a group of Christians in a virtually defunct congregation in a neighbouring area; they then took over that church and brought it to life. In other areas they have arranged for a group of 10–20 Christians to move house and settle together in a new housing estate. These Christians have thus formed a nucleus for a new church in a formerly unevangelised area. Others have then been attracted into their fellowship, neighbours have been won to the Lord and a growing church has resulted. In yet other areas house meetings have been established in the homes of Christians who normally come into the central church by car and these house meetings have grown into full churches with the support of the mother congregation.

In countries where the Christian church was established some centuries ago there is a danger that population movements have left church buildings standing like forlorn monuments in the wrong sites. New housing areas often remain quite unevangelised without any church presence. In the college where I teach we have discovered in neighbouring small towns a variety of housing estates where there is no church and no Christian witness. Student teams are now involved in co-operation with local churches in trying to plant churches in those areas. As a result there is now a firmly established church in a new housing area in Harlow, a struggling new group in a London overspill estate in Hertford and there are further challenges confronting us in near-by villages.

I believe that such church planting is better accomplished by teams of laymen together than by one lone individual on his own. The church as a body can help in this by organising and training such evangelistic teams. Six or eight members could form an effective force. Two may visit homes with the aim of starting a childrens' meeting in some home which is willing to open its doors for this purpose. Two others may visit round in order to establish an adults' home meeting, while other pairs will aim at youth or womens' meetings. As people come to faith in Christ, baptism and the establishment of a church will result.

The task of the clergy in this evangelistic mission will be to discover and mobilise suitable laity for this work – it is the task of the clergy and full-time Christian workers to find leaders. These lay workers will need much encouragement, advice and help. The minister can work alongside in this way.

When my wife and I were in Asia we rejoiced to see teams of Christians moving out from their home towns into the surrounding villages which were still unevangelised. We accompanied these teams from time to time, but not every week. It is important that the missionary should not be seen to be the leader lest local Christians become dependent on his presence. They should be encouraged to develop their own spiritual initiative and sense of responsibility and leadership. This principle applies equally to clergy in this country. From behind the scenes we can help in the ministry of encouragement and training.

Laity can and should plant churches or new outreach meetings.

(b) *The Laity in worship* The Anglican Prayer Book is known as *The Book of Common Prayer;* Archbishop Cranmer's aim in the liturgy was that the whole congregation should be vitally involved in the communal worship. Cranmer wanted to avoid the practice of the Catholic Church at that time, as well as its doctrinal errors. The idea of the priest performing an act of worship which the congregation merely observed was anathema to Cranmer. He rejected the priestly function of the minister and emphasised the priesthood of every believer. In the worship service therefore the whole body of Christ come together in worship, adoration, confession, prayer and humble listening to the Word of God.

People today will not be attracted to services in which they play no participatory role. If they do not become personally involved in the services, there is a grave danger that they will leave the church.

Sadly we have often returned in the Protestant churches to a worship pattern which again emphasises the radical difference between the minister and the laity. Often the minister in solitary fashion performs like a little pope in the front. In some churches the idea of congregational worship has been replaced by the minister doing everything. The congregation merely sing the hymns he commands, stand or sit as directed and say "amen" when the minister finishes praying. Of course the congregation join him in their hearts, so that to some extent he is "leading" in prayer. But in reality the degree of participation is minimal.

Much thought needs to be given to making worship services into times of joint worship which truly reflect our doctrine of the priesthood of all believers. Our services should be so warm and attractive that even newcomers without a church background will rejoice to be a part of them.

In Jewish life the home is the centre of religious worship. Synagogue is primarily where the Scriptures are read and Talmud is studied – hence the Yiddish word for the synagogue stems from the German word for "school". In the home the whole family share in the formalities of worship with humour, lively visual forms and freedom for all to participate with a deep sense of family unity and love. As we noted earlier, our family is now the Church of Jesus Christ where all believers are our brothers and sisters. In moving the location of our worship from the home to the church, let us not lose that freedom to enjoy humour and loving unity as we participate together as a body and as a family in worship.

True worship of this nature will demonstrate many aspects of Christian truth and will therefore develop into a form of proclamation. We want our services to be attractive to outsiders as well as suitable for long established Christians. We are sometimes fearful of change lest we offend our members.

Believers need to be taught the necessity of cultural changes in worship patterns. We must help older Christians to understand the purposes of true worship. Otherwise we are in danger of becoming keepers of aquariums rather than fishers of men.

(c) *The Laity in edification* Paul instructs the Colossian Christians to "teach and admonish one another in all wisdom" (Col. 3:16). Likewise in 1 Thess. 5:14 he urges the brethren to "admonish the idlers, encourage the faint-hearted, help the weak, be patient with them all". All Christians share in mutual responsibility for edifying and admonishing fellow members of the Church. Jesus himself is the chief shepherd and pastor of his flock; ministers are also called to be his under-shep-herds, but this does not exclude the biblical injunction to Christians generally to admonish one another.

Many ministers today are battling to teach their members that a pastoral visit from an elder or some other church member is as good as a visit from the minister himself. Over the centuries we have built up a tradition that only the minister is able to pastor. It takes time and persistent instruction to change centuries-old ideas. Typical of this is Wimborne Parish Church where a group of lay pastors share with the vicar and each is pastorally responsible for some 70–80 church members.

The life of the church would be much enhanced if every Christian felt deep personal responsibility for others in the fellowship. We need each other's encouragement and admonition. In prayer and Bible study together in twos and threes we can strengthen and edify one another.

The layman's ministry of edification will probably be primarily in an unofficial capacity as Christians share together, but those who have the gift of Bible teaching should also be used in the more public ministry of the church.

After the fall of Rome to the barbarian tribes from the north education became increasingly restricted to the ranks of the clergy in Western Europe. This social fact moulded the ministry of the Church, restricting leadership and teaching largely to the clergy. In the Byzantine churches of eastern Europe the position was exactly the reverse. The clergy were largely uneducated and even illiterate, while education and the study of theology lay in the hands of the laity. Orthodox priests performed the external rites of the liturgy. But theological debate and study remained uncloistered.

Os Guinness in a recent talk given at All Nations Christian College on "Modern Consciousness and its moulding power" expounded the danger of the church reacting to social pressures like a chameleon rather than acting on social development as a catalyst. The western Church chameleon failed to teach and train its laity so that they could have a vital ministry within the fellowship of the Church. There were of course some notable exceptions, but generally laymen lay dormant.

Social situations have changed radically today. Widespread education to a high level means that many ordinary church members can read widely in biblical and theological studies. This may be threatening to an insecure minister, but actually gives scope for multiplication and diversification of ministry and leadership.

This in turn allows new organisational patterns to develop in the church, whereby a church can cope with larger numbers without becoming impersonal and failing in pastoral care. If the minister alone shoulders responsibility for all the pastoral and teaching work of the church, the congregation is limited according to the time and ability of the pastor. The church will therefore remain relatively small.

Particularly in the great cities of the world with their vast populations this question of church structures becomes specially important. A church with a thousand members only scratches the surface in a city of a million people. Such a metropolis requires either a multitude of little churches with a thousand or so members; or we should establish a few larger churches with perhaps ten thousand members each. As we noted in the first chapter, larger churches demand structures to match. Laity will have to be leaders in every area of church life.

Let us illustrate from political realities. The Prime Minister of Britain takes ultimate responsibilty for everything in his country, but in practice he has no inkling of what transpires in the village council in Stanstead Abbotts where I live. He governs through his cabinet. Cabinet members each have their own area of responsibility in which they are dependent on a particular branch of the civil service. And so government reaches down through the various levels of delegated responsibility.

Delegated leadership is required in a larger church. Diagram 1 shows the traditional autocratic leadership pattern which has been traditional in western churches. Diagram 2 reflects the shared ministry approach with a board of elders alongside the pastor(s), but together they are still directly responsible for pastoral care of the total membership and all ministry in the church. Diagram 3 demonstrates an approach with delegated leadership which will allow the church to grow to any size. The diagram has only shown three levels (the eldership, area leaders and membership generally), but as the church grows it may require more layers of delegation. Each level of leadership may be vested in one person or it can equally be exercised through the shared leadership of a group.

The large church will find it helpful not only to have communal services on Sunday, but also a multitude of smaller fellowships during the week to foster more intimate fellowship. These will of course be led, taught and

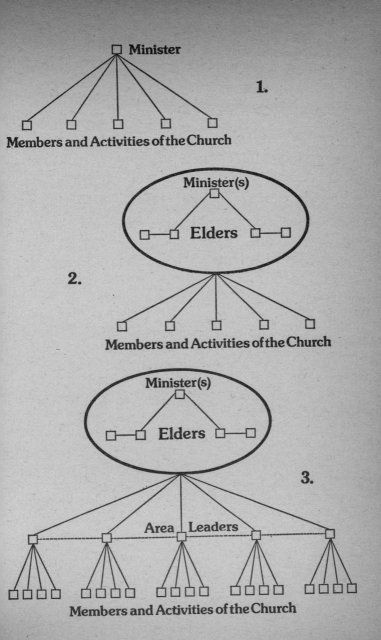

Minister

1.

Members and Activities of the Church

Minister(s)

Elders

2.

Members and Activities of the Church

Minister(s)

Elders

3.

Area Leaders

Members and Activities of the Church

pastored by lay leadership. In such a church the minister(s) and elders become increasingly pastors and trainers of lay leaders rather than having a more widespread ministry to all the membership.

2 *Schism or multiplication*

Growth encourages but presents problems. Church buildings become too small. After some decades of decline in western churches we are encouraged to note many congregations growing apace today. Ten years ago we heard debates about removing pews from half-empty churches, thus making room for bookstalls or other facilities. This remains the problem in some huge and largely redundant churches in run-down city areas, but elsewhere we begin to hear of congregations outgrowing their buildings.

Some while ago I was invited to preach at a church in an old housing area on the outskirts of a large city. There was no parking space. The church building was sardined between private houses. The congregation squeezed into all available space like an overfull tube of toothpaste. I spoke on the biblical call to mission, urging the congregation to share in the Lord's own vision for mission to all peoples, Jews and Gentiles alike. Interest overseas begins with active mission in one's own neighbourhood – and both stem from a biblical view of God's desires for his world and a grateful appreciation of what his salvation means for us.

After the service I went to lunch with a leading elder. He told me that they were in principle interested in evangelism, but there was no practical possibility. The toothpaste tube was full. No more could be accommodated. They had considered the question of enlarging their premises, but that too proved impossible owing to the close proximity of the neighbouring houses.

In the elder's study was a large map of the neighbourhood. He had put pins of different colours into the map according to where the various Christians lived. The pins flourished in three distinct groups. One group stood like sentinels on guard around the church building. A second group was located in a housing area where there was also a lively church of a different denomination. The third cluster of pins lived in a housing estate with no active church in their neighbourhood.

I suggested that they hive off that third cluster from the mother congregation and form a daughter church. This would establish a Christian witness in their locality and would at the same time vacate a few pews for the benefit of others. Evangelism might then make progress.

My friend found the suggestion inconceivable. "Mr. N. lives in that area and he runs our youth programme. And Mr. X. too – he is one of our elders. There are two Sunday school teachers living out there." "Set apart for me Barnabas and Saul for the work to which I have called them," said the Holy Spirit to the five prophets and teachers gathered together in Antioch (Acts 13:2). Could the Antioch church manage without them? Will the milk go sour if you remove some of the cream? No! It merely leaves room at the top of the bottle. Undeveloped gifts of leadership will now be able to flourish among Christians who are at present inactive.

The church did nothing. I was not surprised a year or so later to hear that the church had split over doctrinal quarrels issuing from the charismatic renewal movement. Nearly a third of the membership left the church and founded a new house fellowship in the area we had discussed. But the members of the new fellowship came from all three areas. It would have been better if the division had come through loving consent and had been on geographical, not doctrinal lines. But both groups determined to win new members to their congregation. Evangelism began to take wing.

Division often increases the number of active Christians. Every congregation consists of a nucleus of deeply involved members surrounded by a number of people who attend services but do little else. Division through the planting of daughter churches or house meetings adds to the number of active nuclei. Schism will do the same, but sin may abound and motives for active involvement may be less pure.

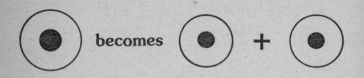

3 *Homogenous units?*

It seems almost like a take-over bid! The streets of London teem with men of every colour and nation. The platforms in the underground station sound like Babel with men of every tongue – it is hard to find a native Englishman among the crowds of tourists, foreign students and immigrants. As I drive to London from my home, I pass through residential areas on the outskirts of the city. One area is largely Pakistani and Bengali;

another is alive with West Indians; yet another is heavy with the black hats, black coats and black beards of a tight-knit Chassidic Jewish community.

London is not unique. Every great city in the world can tell a similar story. Russians and Japanese vie for space with the resident Malays, Indians and Chinese on the over-crowded pavements of Singapore. Nigerians and Cubans sit side by side with Vietnamese and Russians at the university of Odessa. Pakistanis and Indians merge discreetly with Italians on the dusty streets of Libyan towns. Oil-rich Arab states import cheap labour from some countries and skilled expertise from others to supplement their own inadequate labour force in the huge national effort to invest their vast oil revenues in the building of new industries, towns and facilities.

Yes, people all over the world are being forced to jostle one another in the rat-race of life. Although in some cases this leads to a breakdown of racialism and a growth of mutual understanding and international tolerance, in other cases men glare at each other with neither sympathy nor understanding. Racial segregation is practised and national sensitivities flourish. In university refectories Africans sit at one table, Chinese at another, British at others. Isolated Jewish ghettoes in London or New York can be paralleled with remote Mennonite valleys in America or distinct Italian suburbs in Australia. Of course these separated communities are inevitably influenced by the majority culture by which they are surrounded; and they in their turn have some influence on their host country, but only the minority fringes actually merge together. Most people find that life in a foreign country makes them more intensely nationalistic than ever they were in their own countries. Pakistani immigrants can become defensive in staunch insistence on traditional customs, for they feel threatened by their position as a minority. And the Englishman overseas can display a proud assurance that he alone is truly civilised, looking down on foreigners who cannot even make a decent cup of tea!

How does all this affect the structures of the church? The New Testament plainly states that racial barriers are broken down in Christ – "there is no distinction between Jew and Greek" (Rom. 10:12). In the new creation "there cannot be Greek and Jew, circumcised and uncircumcised, barbarian, Scythian, slave, free man" (Col. 3:11). Racial, economic or sex distinctions fade into insignificance in the light of the overriding umbrella fact that we "are all one in Christ Jesus" (Gal. 3:28).

The Book of Revelation dramatically describes the climax of history in the perfection of God's Kingdom. John sees "a great multitude which no man could number, from every nation, from all tribes and peoples and tongues, standing before the throne and before the lamb" (Rev. 7:9). A central feature in Jewish thought concerning the Kingdom was its universality, and we look forward to the fulfilment of this hope. People of all sorts from all nations will be gathered together around the throne to worship the Lord. We not only long for that day because the Lord we love will be given the glory and honour which is his due. We also look forward eagerly to the day when barriers of hatred, suspicion and discrimination will be eliminated.

But in the person of Jesus the Kingdom has already come. We cannot just wait for the final climax of the

Kingdom without beginning to work now for the implementation of its demands. We cannot rest content if the church does not reflect the nature of the Kingdom. In these days of racial antipathies in every area of the world one telling aspect of our witness will be our Christian ability to break through these barriers. Racial tension simmers between Chinese and Malays, Japanese and Koreans, Jews and Arabs, blacks and whites, South American Indians of Amazonia and other Brazilians, etc. In New Testament days antipathy boiled between Jews and Gentiles. With typical pride the Jew saw himself as "*the* people" while others were lumped together as "the nations" – and still today the term "goyim" grates in the ear with a mixture of fear and dislike. What a break-through that in Christ Jew and Gentile come together in loving unity! The lump of today's world desperately needs such a leaven of love.

Although we strive for the biblical vision and goal of ultimate deep Christian unity, we know in practice that churches grow more easily and rapidly if they are homogeneous, consisting of only one race or only one class, caste or educational level. Research would seem to support this view. Chinese fellowships all over the world flourish and multiply, winning to Christ great numbers of fellow Chinese nurses, students and other overseas Chinese. Their zeal for evangelism and their love for the Lord challenge us all. The character of such a homogeneous group attracts the non-Christian Chinese who feels at home with them.

In like manner Hebrew congregations and Messianic Synagogues have sprung up with new verve and energy through the less traditional "Jews for Jesus" movement in America. The Jew can enjoy the freedom of such totally Jewish congregations where he does not have to moderate his somewhat poignant humour and his very black-and-white speech to fit in with his Gentile neighbours' love for such words as "somewhat", "rather" and "possibly".

In Africa and Asia too the churches or congregations are often organised along racial lines. In Kenya dioceses may follow tribal lines. In Malaysia entirely Indian churches will have no contact with totally Chinese congregations just a few hundred yards away down the road. Where we worked in Indonesia most of the churches were restricted in practice to one race only.

In Britain too white churches have made little impact on their West Indian neighbours. Black Sunday schools flourish in English churches, for West Indian immigrants come from a strongly religious background at home and therefore desire their children to have instruction in the Christian faith. But they themselves do not feel at home in white churches. West Indian Pentecostal churches however show remarkable growth, attracting large numbers to their meetings.

Monochrome churches of this nature can stem from ill-disguised racial prejudice. Where that is the case, we must deplore it. The Christian Gospel utterly rejects such attitudes and must be seen publicly to have broken down any such sinful antagonism. Otherwise the witness of the Christian Church is badly tarnished.

However, not all homogeneous groupings in the Church have such bad motives. Language barriers may prevent united worship. In our town in Malaysia there were ten or twelve separate congregations using different languages. This was a tragedy in a situation where the Christian Church was a tiny minority. It would have been greatly advantageous if the approximately 500 Protestant Christians could have met together in fellowship and worship, but no practical possibility presented itself. In our area of Indonesia too churches ran along the lines of language divisions. Although there was good fellowship and co-operation between the various churches, these divisions were perpetuated even in the big cities where all the different races spoke the national language of Indonesia.

Often the prime cause for such homogeneous groupings is cultural. People feel more at home with others of their own background. Although status distinctions and barriers of dislike are broken down in Christ, making us all one in him, yet still basic distinctions exist. Jews are still Jews and Greeks are still Greeks; men are still men and women remain as feminine as ever. Cultural differences therefore continue to exist, enriching the life of the body.

The various races in the Church will enjoy and even need separate gatherings from time to time to discuss together the particular issues they face, to express themselves in their own particular approaches to worship and just to enjoy a fellowship which does not require cultural adjustment all the time. Thus the Chinese fellowships have particular approaches to the Christian faith because of the enormous influence of Confucian thought on all Chinese. Their attitude to Scripture is moulded by this background, which also makes certain types of sermons or messages more popular than others. They also have their own special battles to face which may not be relevant to other races – problems of food offered to ancestral spirits, attitudes to Buddhist funerals, the binding effects of having been offered as a child to the Goddess of Mercy or some other spirit.

Non-Christians may not yet have overcome racial pride and prejudice. Anti-white bitterness may still eat like a cancer in some African hearts. Europeans on the other hand may swagger in assumed superiority. Both attitudes may prevent people from hearing the good news of Jesus Christ through people of other races. They may need to be evangelised through homogeneous groupings which only present the scandal of the Cross without the further stumbling-block of racial issues. People like to become Christians without crossing racial, linguistic or class barriers. But those who come to follow Christ in true discipleship through such racially monochrome meetings must not be allowed to remain in attitudes of pride, bitterness or insularity. They must be taught that we *are* all one in Christ – and this teaching needs to come not only verbally, but also in the practice of church life.

In the summer of 1977 a colloquium was held in Pasadena on the subject of the "Homogeneous Unit Principle". An agreed statement was issued after the discussions which has been published by Scripture Union under the title *Explaining the Gospel in Today's World*. This states: "We have found considerable help in the concept of change. To acknowledge the fact of homogeneous units is not to acquiesce in the characteristics they possess which are displeasing to Christ . . . we wish also to affirm that homogeneous units can change and must always change. For Christ the Lord gives to his people new standards. They also receive a new homogeneity which transcends all others, for now they find their essential unity in Christ, rather than in culture." The report concludes with the great vision of the ultimate future when all peoples will worship the Lord together. We are therefore "called to anticipate on earth the life of heaven, and thus to develop both cultural richness and heterogeneous fellowship". I feel this strongly in the college where I teach. What a delight to see Jews and Germans, South African whites and blacks, Indians and Pakistanis in deep fellowship together!

Thus far we have talked only of racially homogeneous groupings. However, other distinctions can also divide us. Caste, class or educational and financial differences may prove equally problematic. India has legally abolished caste distinctions and many more modern and educated city dwellers sense a desire to be free from them. But old ways enmesh them like octopus tentacles. Can the church cut through the tentacles with its knives of love? The crunch often comes in questions of marriage – can the Christian marry someone of different caste? Failure stalks many churches, but joyfully new attitudes are seeping into the Church through the gracious and patient proddings of the Holy Spirit.

In Britain class barriers still rear their ugly heads. The church in the stockbroker belt finds it hard to relate to the council housing estate on the edge of the town. One church I know has found it necessary to have different youth meetings – one for those who speak Oxford English and a second one for children of more working-class backgrounds. The Church has been re-thinking evangelism in the poorer and rougher areas of our cities during these past ten years or more. Much is being done through centres like Shrewsbury House or the Mayflower Centre: likewise there are a number of churches which are beginning to relate more effectively to a less middle-class culture. We are aware of the dangers of an inverted snobbery – a 100 per cent middle-class church is despised, while an equally homogeneous working-class church will be admired; but we rejoice at every sign of the British church reaching out to all classes and types of people. But the struggle to reach every segment of society is only just beginning. Can the church be built with bricks of different classes sharing together?

In one village I know they rejoice in having Christians of various educational backgrounds. Thus home meetings display the whole spectrum. In their mens' discussion groups half a dozen of them range from good university degrees and theological qualifications to folk without any academic background. Discussions are rich in variety, but can also be frustrating – the intellectuals' questions bore the others, while the approaches of the practical working men fail to answer the searchings of the teachers. But in a small village with a mere handful of active Christians they need to love one another and work together in true fellowship. The church with its emphasis on sermons and reading of an intellectual nature often fails to take into account those who are less educated. It is a challenge to us to make sure that we cater for all levels of education and encourage our church to reflect the glories of heaven where men of all educational backgrounds will worship together.

The Corinthian church and the Christians to whom James wrote had problems too. The rich and the poor found sharing in loving equality a difficult task. In Pakistan most of the Christians are rather poor and it is hard for wealthier folk to feel at home in their midst. In the English-speaking churches of South Africa the reverse holds true. The title of a German novel, *Clothes make People*, sadly speaks to the reality of the situation. The fur coat or the smartly tailored suit finds it hard to rub its elegant shoulders with less dainty apparel. Both feel embarrassed in the presence of the other.

How therefore do we structure our churches to reflect the need for homogeneous gatherings for evangelism as well as for fellowship without losing that necessary heterogeneous nature which is not only a reflection of the Kingdom of God, but is also a telling witness in this age of racial, cultural and class divisions?

Various churches have experimented with united Sunday services and separated mid-week meetings. The Sunday services will need of course to vary from week to week, allowing the different component parts of the church to be central. West Indian singing will alternate with the hymns of Wesley. While most can share together relatively easily in worship, prayer and testimony, there may be greater difficulty with the sermon. This may need to be kept brief and punchy, leaving the more developed expositions and meaty teaching for those who can digest it mid-week. For some, one simple verse may be all they can manage at one time – a national Christian leader from the Sind Desert region told me that he gave local Christians one new verse per month! For those who require and can digest more thorough teaching of the whole counsel of God the house meetings will provide stimulus. These mid-week gatherings can be graded and varied according to the needs of the people present. They may vary in membership along lines of race, education, class, age or any other question.

So the church in one way or another will want to cater for the varied needs of its membership by supplying homogeneous groupings. These will also be the primary centres for evangelistic activity to introduce the non-Christian to the message of Christ in a milieu in which he feels at home. But the church will also want to introduce its members to the radically new and heavenly life where all racial and cultural animosities begin to give way to the love of God. Professor Lane in his *New London Commentary* on Mark defines the content of the evangel in the ancient world as "an historical event which introduces a new situation for the world". That remains true for us today. If our Gospel is to be truly good news for the strife-torn world of our age it must demonstrate not only that "God is love" (1 John 4:8), but also that his life in us produces a new love for our brothers and sisters in Christ. John himself states this baldly and categorically: "he who does not love does not know God" (1 John 4:8). This is Jesus' new commandment to his followers that we "love one another" (John 13:34). It is striking to see this working out in the church in Antioch where the black Symeon shares with the other four prophets and teachers in apparent harmony (Acts 13:1). All five came from very different backgrounds, but they were together as one united group of the Lord's servants.

Such love in heterogeneous churches will play a part in drawing men to the Lord and thus will contribute to the growth of the church.

4 FACTORS IN EVANGELISTIC METHOD

1 *Win the winnables!*

Dr. McGavran has emphasised the need to re-educate western Christians to understand that there are enormous opportunities today for churches to grow. "We face a most responsive world," he affirms with the added statement that there are "more winnable people in the world than ever before."

It is true that many Christians have lost the vision that churches can increase numerically at a fast rate. When I returned to Britain from Indonesia for our first leave, I was often introduced in church meetings with an air of depression. "We are always pleased to have a missionary in our midst," the church secretary would announce, "for the missionary is to us an example of faithful perseverance. Despite many years of hard work in an unresponsive field he has not been deterred by fruitlessness." Such introductions were embarrassing, for the work in North Sumatra had been exceedingly fruitful. Multitudes had come to Christ, and changed lives were a normal part of the regular work there. (See Elizabeth Goldsmith's *God Can be Trusted*.) We soon felt that it was a vital part of our deputation ministry therefore to encourage British Christians that the God of Indonesia is also alive and wanting to work in Britain too.

Since these years the mood of the British church has changed quite markedly. Many churches are growing steadily and some are increasing very fast indeed. The wide and deep influence of the charismatic renewal movement has also given many in the church a new faith in a God who works in power. As a result young people are singing with joyful confidence "All over the world the Spirit is moving." A moment's consideration will show of course that such a chorus is more a hopeful statement of faith than of visible reality. Some areas of the world evidence tremendous vitality in the Christian Church with large numbers of people coming to repentance and faith in Christ; but other countries and regions seem rock-like in resistance to the claims of Jesus Christ.

But these are days when many people in a variety of different countries are hungry for spiritual life and are therefore open to the message of Christ. We do not want to fall into a trite triumphalism, but likewise we cannot ignore the wide open doors which are presented to us today. McGavran talks in terms of the "winnable" and parallels this to the medical concept of "curable". He maintains that the Holy Spirit is so working in some societies and in some individuals that they are now in the position of being "winnable". Others are still resistant to the Gospel. Is it this distinction which was in Paul's mind when he asked the Colossian Christians to pray that God would "open to us a door for the word" (Col. 4:3)?

Wesley affirmed that "it is the task of the Christian to bend his back to second the work of the blessed Holy Spirit". Where the Spirit is obviously at work, there we should be present as "fellow workers with God" (1 Cor. 3:9, 2 Cor. 6:1). McGavran's parallel picture of "curable" is illustrative of his views. If a country has ample doctors for every possible medical ministry, then it can well afford to dedicate some of them to the comforting and loving task of easing the sufferings of the incurable terminal patient. But if there is such a shortage of medical personnel that only a minority of patients can possibly obtain any attention at all, then it would seem wiser to concentrate the doctors on those patients who could be healed. This is of course the situation in many Third World countries and it causes untold heartache and pangs of conscience to the conscientious doctor.

I remember going to a small township in New Zealand with a total population of about 200 people. The village had three churches, each of which had its own minister to care for its handful of members. What luxury! Or was it superfluity? I had just come from an area of south-east Asia where multitudes were hungry for the Gospel and where I had frequently been greeted with comments like: "if someone would come to my village, we would turn to Christ." Should such openness be a determining factor in the placing of personnel or even in personal guidance?

The Church Growth movement therefore unashamedly supports a concentration of the Church's resources in personnel and money on those peoples and areas where a fruitful harvest can be gathered with relative ease. Thus Roy Shearer in his *Wildfire: Church Growth in Korea*, states emphatically: "we should concentrate our limited forces on areas where there is response. This will mean thinning our personnel for church extension in the nonresponsive areas, since our forces are limited, but the result will be more church growth in both areas. It is a sinful waste to keep two areas equally staffed just because there is the same number of citizens in each, when there is a great difference in potential for growth of the Church. If we say we must do our best to aid growth in the non-responsive area, thereby holding back resources from a church-growing area, we deceive ourselves."

This sort of approach will prove a healthy corrective to former inefficiency in the Christian Church with its lack of real vision and concern for the growth of God's Church, but it also presents us with a variety of problems. Despite the positive lessons we may learn from such strategic thinking, we may be led to question whether it is not somewhat simplistic in its pragmatic emphasis on numerical success.

(a) *Strategic placing of personnel* The Church Growth movement is critical of the frequent failure of the Christian Church to give priority to the numerical increase of the Church and thus also our failure to locate our personnel in what they consider a strategic manner.

There is little doubt that we are befogged by clouds of ignorance. We may have great debates on evangelistic methods and strategy, but we often have little accurate information on which to base our discussions. Most of us are unsure how fast our churches are growing or even perhaps whether they are growing at all. We are not confident how to measure such growth – by church membership? Or by baptismal figures? Or by attendance at Sunday services or at the Lord's Supper? Or should holiness and prayerfulness be taken into account and thus growth be measured perhaps by attendance at prayer meetings?

Church Growth people talk much of the relative openness of one segment of the population in comparison with others – i.e. one class may be more responsive to the Gospel than another. Or it may be a question of generation, race or educational standard. But we may not really be very sure what sort of people attend churches or in what sections of the population conversions are actually taking place. People criticise the western churches for being largely middle class – that may be our impression, but would statistics bear this out? And what is meant by "middle class"? Others may criticise the church for appealing largely to the elderly with little attraction for the younger generation or for young marrieds. But one wonders whether the facts would support this impression.

It is not just a question of what sort of people we already have in our churches. Perhaps a more important area of research is to discover what sort of people are becoming Christians and therefore what sections of the population are most open to the Gospel of Christ.

If we knew these things more accurately and had the growth of the Church as a major priority in our thinking, then we might be compelled to change our ideas on where our ministers, missionaries and active lay Christians should locate themselves and in what spheres of ministry they should be busy. Again we are forced back to the question of whether our ministry is to be *primarily* the nurturing of fish already in the aquarium or on the other hand the calling to be fishers of men with the aim on church growth numerically.

Eyes can also be blinded to the question of church growth by the happy situation of a full church. Good Bible-teaching churches in the cities will usually attract Christians from the whole city to sit at the feet of spiritually-minded expositors of the Scriptures. Students and young professionals will frequently flock to such a church to feed on the quality teaching provided. This may play a vital part in the up-building of such Christians and in the long run may therefore contribute to the growth of the Church worldwide through sending out well taught and trained men and women to other areas of our country and abroad. Nevertheless a question mark can hover over such a church. Are people being added to the church through conversion from non-Christian backgrounds or not? Are the Christians therefore being given a vision for evangelism which is fuelled by the encouraging experience of actually seeing people being brought to a knowledge of Christ and themselves being used by the Lord to lead their friends to a personal knowledge of their Saviour?

Many of our larger city churches have enormous potential for growth if the ministers could only catch this vision and devote their energies to fostering it. It is inspiring to visit a church with 500–1,000 well taught members, many of whom in their professional lives demonstrate leadership abilities. If each member brought one new person a year to know the Lord, the explosion of the church would be exciting.

We have been talking of workers within churches

without considering the possibility that God might want them to be located elsewhere. Potential for church growth might be greater in other areas of the same town, in a totally different part of the country or even in another country altogether.

As we saw from Shearer's book on Korea, Church Growth advocates would want people to be located according to church growth possibilities. This could be managed if all Christian workers were under strict authority. Roman Catholic religious orders can move their members at will, for their people are accustomed to following an oath of obedience. This allows them to place their people according to agreed strategy, although there will still be a limit to their freedom in this respect. They too are subject to problems in obtaining visas if they want to move members from one country to another – and their members also take time to learn new languages and cultures, just as do our Protestant workers. The spiritual gifts and talents of their people may also not always fit the situation in the area to which the leaders may want to assign them. So even in Roman Catholic orders there is some limitation to the possibility of moving people to fit in with strategic planning. People are not mere pawns to be moved indiscriminately around God's chessboard. Strategic planning without careful consideration of the welfare of the individual will produce problems. Protestant mission leaders too are well aware of the dangers of persuading their members to slot into urgent vacancies just because there is no one else free to do the job. Round pegs in square holes lead to frustrations, discontent and wasted gifts.

In practice Protestant leaders are not free to move their personnel at will. Vicars have their freehold; Free Church ministers often follow a congregational pattern in which they are not subject to the authority of leaders; missionaries are strongly aware of God's personal guidance to them individually and will not generally be happy meekly and blindly to follow their leaders' directions; lay Christians too cannot be directed autocratically by church leaders as to what their work should be in the world and where they should practise their profession.

There are strong reasons why each of these three categories of people will not always adjust their work or the place of their work to fit the demands of church strategy.

i *Ministers* Vicars and ministers do not always plan the development of their ministries to aim at maximum church growth. Sadly we have developed almost a hierarchy of churches. There is virtually a sense of promotion as a minister heads towards the recognised "plum" churches. I was recently most encouraged to talk with a successful minister who had built up a largely stagnant church until it became a well-known flourishing congregation where many people had come to follow the Lord. Having spent some years in achieving this, he had now resigned and moved to a sleepy little church in a small town where there was little vital witness for Christ. This small town is also in an area where the churches are mostly in decline. He was offered positions in various large churches around the country, but he feels that his calling is to make churches grow. His prayer therefore is that his new ministry will also see evidence of the work of the Spirit in the growth of the church.

My friend described to me the run-down condition of his future house, and implied that his finances would suffer from this move. Sadly, housing and finance often play an unduly important part in determining the movements of many full-time workers. This can be further linked to the danger of settling into a comfortable rut as the years pass. It is a natural tendency in middle age and beyond to dislike the thought of moving with all the disruption and discomfort involved. If one is contentedly settled in a reasonably happy situation, the temptation is to remain there too long. Ministers' work is stifled by having been too long in one church without the stimulus of new challenges. And the world map is dotted with the wrecks of churches whose development has been strangled by the unduly long stay of their minister. How one sympathises; they do not want to hurt him by telling him that they need a new approach from a new man. And often they themselves are not aware of their needs, for they are contented in relative stagnation. Likewise it takes real courage and self-sacrifice for the minister to take the plunge and move on to a new situation with new people and a new ministry. But the healthy growth of our churches is and must remain our aim.

ii *Missionaries* Missionaries too can dig their heels in and refuse to be moved. Most missionaries have had to move very frequently in the early years of their life overseas, so they generally are less tempted by the subtle desire for a quiet rut. Every few years they have to uproot from their home and adopted country in order to return to their native land for furlough. Moving home is an accepted part of their lives. They have grown used to constantly facing new situations and learning to know new people.

Nevertheless they too can prove inflexible. Their call to a particular people or place can become ossified, so that they are unwilling to hear the voice of God moving them on. Many forget that guidance comes one step at a time.

In our own experience we felt sure that God had called us to work in Indonesia, but after a couple of years he moved us on. For political reasons it proved impossible to return there after our first furlough. Later we were settled into a particular ministry in Singapore, but again the Lord moved us on although we had been sure we had been in God's place for us. So he prepared us for our present position in a British training college.

The Lord's call is like giving travel instructions. You tell the driver to take the road to Manchester. He thinks he is going to stay on that road until he reaches his destination, but after a while new instructions are given. "Take the road to the left, sign-posted 'Crewe'." Now he thinks that Crewe is his goal, but actually there may be a couple more little turns before he actually arrives. God's direction to each stage of our life may be just the introduction to his next step for us. We should not become so deeply entrenched in our positions that he cannot move us on.

The American Baptists in Nellore, India saw less than a hundred people becoming Christians in their first twenty-five years work. But in 1865 a new missionary, John Clough, came to the area and by 1878 there were

12,806 people baptised. The first missionaries had concentrated on the high caste Hindus. Clough observed that they were largely resistant to the Christian message, while the despised Madigas could be more receptive. It was therefore through his move to a different caste that the church began to grow fast.

When my wife and I were working in Malaysia, one of our fellow missionaries caused considerable controversy. He had worked for many long years in isolated and resistant Hakka Chinese villages. He had gained a good knowledge of the Hakka dialect of Chinese and also of Hakka culture. But the work in these villages was exceedingly unrewarding. He was then offered the position of pastor of a key English-speaking church in the capital town of that particular state. It was a strategic position and he accepted the post. Some of his fellow missionaries felt that he had abandoned the call of God, failing to persevere in rugged and largely unfruitful work. Had he just given up a tough work in favour of a soft option? Or had he moved from an unfruitful ministry to a key strategic position? Certainly the following years vindicated his choice, for that church came to new life and many people were added to the church. In fact, more Hakka Chinese were converted through this English-speaking church in the town than through his long years in the villages.

How hard it can be too for a missionary to be open to the possibility that God might call him to return to his home country! After some years overseas he no longer feels at home in Britain. As the years progress he may well have lost many of his friends and it is possible too that he will no longer have any family alive.

Unwillingness on the part of the missionary may be further compounded by criticisms from other people, who assume that a missionary call must be for life. But the western Church has much to learn from the churches overseas and it is quite possible that God will be sending some overseas for a few years in order to learn lessons which can then be brought back to the home church.

iii *Laity* I was deeply challenged some years ago when visiting the Christian Union at the University of Singapore. I met there some students who were meeting regularly as a small group to pray together how best to invest their lives for the advance of the Gospel. They agreed that it was right for them to practise their professions rather than go into the ordained ministry. The question now was where to work. They became increasingly convicted of the need of the neglected and rather backward east coast of Peninsular Malaysia. So, after qualifying, they all went to various little towns along that beautiful coastline to practise as doctors, dentists, teachers and nurses. It seemed like professional suicide. The east coast was where all the worst teachers and medics stagnated, if they could not get a job anywhere else. Facilities were poor and promotion unlikely.

But what was their aim in life? To serve or to gain promotion, position and financial reward? They gave a professional service in those areas which was something quite new. For the first time people could visit a doctor or dentist who took a loving interest in them as people and cared thoughtfully for them.

As a result of their work in those small coastal towns,

little churches have sprung up all along the coast. Previously there had been a church in a larger town, but nothing much elsewhere.

Sadly our laity in the west often lack that sort of vision for service and for the expansion of the Church. Many only think in terms of professional advancement and that determines where they should live. Some look for a good church and then try to find a job nearby How many look for evangelistic need and for churches which desperately require their help before deciding where to pitch their tents?

Watchman Nee had his own peculiar strategy for evangelism. He would encourage groups of families together to move to an area and thus establish a church as a Christian testimony. People would thus not only hear the preaching of the Gospel from the lips of a solitary witness, but they would see a Christian community in their life together. This also obviates the perennial problem of loneliness. Man is made for fellowship. The lone pioneer needs to be unusually rugged in spiritual and psychological stamina.

I know of one church in Britain which has encouraged groups of its members to move to a particular place in order together to establish a living church there. The South American Missionary Society has found that it is better to start a new pioneer work with a whole team of workers going together with a variety of different gifts and ministries to contribute to the new venture. Such a team makes a much deeper impression on a town than any one couple could do on their own. The workers also enjoy the supportive fellowship of each other.

Strategic placing of personnel can play a vital part in the advancement of the Gospel and in the growth of God's Church. There are problems in this thought and God in his wisdom often overrules our man-made strategies, but nevertheless each one of us individually and the Church as a body should be trying to relate the guidance of God's Spirit to an overall strategy of mission.

(b) *A swamped church?* The Church Growth movement tells us that personnel should be placed according to the openness of a situation. To some extent this is valid strategy, but it sometimes fails to take into account the negative influence of too many outsiders.

Small churches or Christian Unions can feel overwhelmed when a large crowd of outside Christians of experience and with charisma descend upon them. Local leadership potential can be nipped in the bud, leaving all responsibility to these competent invaders.

In the village where I live there has been a growing openness to Christian things over the past few years. Many total non-Christians have therefore been quite willing for their children to come to a holiday club in the church. This was run by a student from outside. Because he was the only outsider he had to share the work with local Christians, although they had never before done anything of this nature. As a result, they are now leading in all sorts of other activities in the church, particularly the work among children. If the student had brought a team of other competent workers with him, we would not have seen local leadership develop in this way.

Because the majority of the holiday club leadership

was in the hands of local Christians, the character and atmosphere of the work was of a village nature. Children and their parents felt at ease and enjoyed it. Missionaries would have called this an "indigenous mission policy" – and they would be right! In the west we sometimes forget to apply mission policies to our own situations. We have to remember that most of our clergy and "full-time" workers are also temporary outsiders whose ministry is in many ways parallel to that of a missionary overseas. In the very fluid society of cities the minister may stay in the town as long as most of his parishioners, but in smaller places and villages he remains "not quite one of us". When we first moved to the village where we now live, someone talked to us of the "new vicar" – he had in fact been vicar here for almost ten years!

Student Christians may also feel swamped and their leadership potential stifled if too many trained workers come into their midst to exploit the undoubted fruitfulness of student ministry. In colleges and universities where sandwich courses disrupt the possibility of continuity in leadership, there we may be wise to inject stability through permanent leaders who are not students. But in other tertiary education establishments we shall be unwise to introduce too many outsider leaders, unless they are men with the grace and humility to be backroom advisers encouraging the development of spiritual maturity and leadership among the students themselves.

Overseas too there is always a danger of flooding fruitful mission areas with too many expatriate personnel. This will not only swamp the local church, but it will also give the Christian Gospel a foreign taste in the mouths of the national population. The latter has begun to be a major problem in Indonesia of recent years. Stories of revival and mass movement have excited the Christian world. Big-time evangelists rushed to join in collecting the spoils. It makes a marvellous story for mission magazines which in turn will move people to send in the dollars! Too many overseas personnel can damage the local church, unless they are very wise in keeping a low profile. This is particularly true in sensitive Muslim situations.

On one occasion I talked with the elder in charge of a church overseas. He was a godly national Christian and said to me that his church was of course basically for missionaries. I objected and emphasised that it should be geared primarily for the local people. He then informed me that there were more missionaries than national Christians in this church and therefore it was only right that it should cater for the majority by means of a very western approach. The church lived under the shadow of a large mission hospital with a crowd of overseas workers. The healthy development of an indigenous church was badly affected by an excess of missionaries in comparison with the number of national believers.

With some truth it is sometimes said that missionaries are like manure. Spread thinly it is enriching, but in large quantities together it stinks!

(c) *"Shake off the dust."* One of the Indonesian church elders came to our home in some perplexity. He had read again the biblical injunction not to "throw your pearls before swine" (Matt. 7:6) and to "shake off the dust from your feet" (Matt. 10:14) "if people will not receive you or listen to your words". He explained to me that he had paid three visits to a neighbouring small town which had never before had the Gospel preached there. He visited the local coffee shop where the men would gather of an evening and had talked with them about Christ, but as a result of these visits "only about thirty men" had been converted. He wondered whether it was right to continue working in such an unresponsive place! I had to encourage him and explain that in my country such a situation would have been written up in the Christian press as a revival!

It is easy in the cool pages of a book to describe some situations as "hard" or "unresponsive" while designating others as "open" or "fruitful". But these terms are relative. It sounds convincing to talk in terms of concentrating our resources on the more fruitful opportunities, but should this church elder have abandoned this piece of evangelism to which the Lord had called him? There might have been other towns where the harvest would have been greater for that area of North Sumatra was abundantly receptive to the Gospel at that time. And if it did seem right for him to move elsewhere, how long should he first persevere in the first small town? If such a policy were followed logically, then relatively unresponsive countries like Britain or Australia should be almost denuded of Christian workers – I doubt if many of us would really like that!

Many today look at Indonesia with some spiritual envy. We know that there are many problems, but we should love to be in the sort of situation where conversions may fall into your hands like ripe plums. We love to hear the encouraging stories of growth not only in Indonesia, but also in Chile and Brazil, Nigeria and Uganda, Indians in South Africa and Jews in America. But sometimes we forget that today's rich harvest is built on the foundation of former years of hard slog and suffering.

David Bentley-Taylor has movingly described in his *Weathercock's Reward* the long struggle of Bruckner, the pioneer missionary from Germany to Java, the main island of Indonesia. Years of lonely and unrewarding work led to the translation and finally to the distribution of the Scriptures. In the course of his long and fruitless years his missionary society instructed him to move to China because that great country was then opening and people there were receptive. When he refused and stayed firmly in his "hard" situation, his mission disowned him. It was through his translation of the Scriptures that the first men were converted and the great churches of Java were first planted. The present very fruitful mission work in Java owes its life to the perseverance of this one man.

The history of the Church through the centuries is full of similar stories of men who have battled on through disappointment and resistance until finally God has given the break-through. Sometimes this has taken more than one generation of workers to accomplish, so that the first pioneers have died without seeing fruit from their labours. This applies not only to pioneer mission in Africa or Asia, but also to some of the early missionary work which laid the foundations for the spread of the Gospel in Europe in former centuries.

How then do we balance faithful perseverance with

obedience to the biblical injunction to "shake off the dust"? There is no simple answer.

Although the Church Growth movement encourages us to concentrate our resources on responsive situations and people, it does also have a policy with regard to hard segments of the population and resistant areas of the world.

i *Is it really hard?* When faced with an unresponsive situation we should re-examine the strategy of our work. Are we perhaps aiming at the wrong segment of the population? If we worked amongst a different race or class, would we find doors opening in a new way?

ii *Surround them!* In John's Gospel the Word is always accompanied by miraculous signs that demonstrate visibly the truths of the word. Educational experts these days assure us that the "eye-gate" is a vital companion to the "ear-gate". So the verbal preaching of the Gospel carries more conviction if accompanied by visual signs. These may be in the form of miracles, but the reality of the Christian message may also be evidenced by the sign of God at work in changing lives and establishing living churches.

It may therefore be good policy to surround resistant people with live churches where they can see the reality and relevance of the Christian faith. Paul sees the validity of this approach and uses it to justify his own ministry as apostle to the Gentiles. "Inasmuch then as I am an apostle to the Gentiles, I magnify my ministry in order to make my fellow Jews jealous" (Rom. 11:14). This does not negate the validity of direct mission to Jews, as Karl Barth suggested, but it does show that mission to unresponsive peoples may require us to work first among other peoples with the aim of bringing the Gospel in power to those who until now have been resistant. So surround hard people with living churches: don't just hit your head endlessly against brick walls!

Many in Britain today are facing the uphill struggle of evangelising communities who have never experienced living Christian faith in their midst. It is hard for them to conceive the possibility of lives centred on love for God. Others of us are working in churches which for long years have coasted through life in neutral gear. For them too it is hard to imagine what it means to be alive in Christ and consecrated to his service. Such situations can prove very resistant to the renewing work of the Spirit of Christ, but the growth of lively churches in neighbouring areas can open their eyes and stimulate them to new life. Thus a sleepy village situation may be awakened by the sight of a newly enlivened church in the near-by town where people accept new approaches more easily.

The same principle applies to renewal within a congregation. The more traditional membership may find it hard to receive new ideas and new life, but an influx of lively new converts may encourage them to embark on new adventures in Christ. Of course some will feel threatened and resist change, but others will welcome it. A few years ago in North-East England one church experienced new growth when various young married couples were converted, came into the church and enthusiastically revolutionised the rather traditional mid-week prayer meeting and Bible study. In their enthusiasm they offended some, but their vibrant enjoyment of the Lord was infectious. Since then the church has continued to flourish and grow.

But this theory still has problems. Often the existence of a flourishing church in one segment of the population makes no impression at all on other people. Thus a middle-class church may have no impact at all on artisan workers in their immediate neighbourhood. White churches may not in any way affect the thinking of immigrants in the same street. Vibrant but uneducated Pentecostal churches in a Chilean city may leave their wealthier and more educated co-citizens unmoved. A strong church in one African tribe may not impress a neighbouring Muslim tribe at all.

Audrey Fahrni's book *No Turning Back* has an interesting cover. It shows a series of unyielding black lines against which mission arrows are cast. Most turn dejectedly back, but one strong red arrow perseveres and finally makes a small dent in the lower lines, although it totally fails to penetrate the others. Might it not be better, if at all possible, to surround those hard black lines with the encircling witness of live churches?

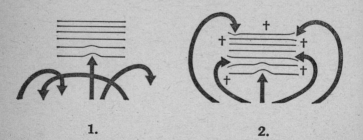

1.　　　　　　2.

This strategy can be helpful. The conversion of non-religious Jews opens the door to the possibility of breaching the defences of more Orthodox relations. The conversion of nominal Muslims gives the lie to the standard Muslim idea that it is impossible for them to consider changing their religion. "Muslims don't ever become Christians," they assure us with bland confidence.

In the very north of Sumatra live the fanatically Muslim Aceh people. Direct evangelistic work among them would be suicidal. Some years ago however six Aceh men stood outside a Chinese church in their town and watched the people leaving the Sunday service. They were struck by the joyful love exhibited on the faces of the Chinese believers. The following Sunday they watched the faces again. They were so impressed that they went to talk with the minister afterwards. Happily he and they could both speak some of the national language and could therefore communicate together. He told them about Jesus. They were converted that morning and fled from the area that same day.

While one rejoices in such vivid stories of personal conversions, many today are querying a strategy which robs the community of an on-going witness in its midst. These six men enjoyed the glory of salvation in Christ, but they could not stay amongst their own people to share what they had experienced. Later in this chapter we shall discuss the possibility of groups of men turning together to Jesus Christ and thus forming a Christian community within the Muslim society. In at least one country individual baptisms are strongly discouraged from among the Muslim group population, for the church advises them to wait until a larger group may be baptised together. They also adapt the external forms of the church to enable it to fit easily into the Muslim environment. Like their Muslim neighbours the Christians also fast, have ritual lustrations before prayer, worship with body movements parallel to Muslim prayer and even pray in the direction of Jerusalem like Daniel (Dan. 6:10).

If we can plant a living testimony around a people or, even better, in their very midst, this may prove a better approach than direct confrontation with a strongly resistant people.

iii *"Watch and pray"* While Church Growth leaders may stress the deployment of personnel according to openness, yet they also say that small teams of workers should be placed in resistant areas to keep watch on the situation. They will then be able to notice if social factors lead to a change of attitude among the people. They will therefore be able to keep the Church informed, so that we can reallocate workers to meet the opportunity when doors begin to open more readily. This "watching" ministry may offer little scope for specific verbal witness, but it will afford special detailed understanding which will motivate us to more urgent and heart-felt prayer.

Such small teams of Christians in hard situations will hopefully give a wide-spread impression that Christians are good people and that the Christian faith is therefore a religion to be respected. When the time comes that people begin to be searching for an alternative to their present atheism or non-Christian religion, the Christian Gospel will be the natural option to be examined first.

Critics may query the use of the Gethsemane words "watch and pray" to describe the ministry of these small groups of Christian witnesses in hard and unresponsive areas – and certainly it is not exactly what Jesus meant by these words! But this does not invalidate the idea of this strategy. Christian workers in closed Muslim lands often sense deep frustration as they ply their professional trades with little or no opportunity to share the message of Christ which burns in their hearts. The truth that God has called them to those professions and they are *in themselves* valid expressions of Christian service is often not satisfying in practice. It may help if they see the strategic role they are playing in keeping watch on the situation for us all, leading us all in the ministry of prayer and spreading among their Muslim friends a general impression of the attractiveness of Christ. This may prove almost equally true in some hard industrial sections of our British community.

(d) *No bed of roses* But perhaps the greatest controversy with regard to this whole question of "winning the winnables" is due to what appears to be an undue emphasis on numerical success. Little or no mention is made of the glory of God through the sanctified lives of his disciples who persevere without seeing much visible success. Statistically, measurable numerical growth takes clear precedence over holiness and sanctification. In the denigration of faithful perseverance in barren mission work there is the danger of ignoring clear biblical teaching. John's Gospel shows the ministry of Jesus constantly rejected by the multitudes, while only a relatively small minority follow him. Again and again in the Lord's ministry he rejects and discourages shallow discipleship. As a result, not only does the rich young ruler turn sadly away, but also the majority of those who had considered themselves to be his disciples (John 6:66). Facile discipleship was ruthlessly shattered by Jesus' descriptions of the cost of following him and by his refusal to tone down what his disciples called "hard sayings" (John 6:60).

Church Growth people tend to emphasise that teaching and "perfecting" comes after entry into the Church. Thus the Great Commission only talks of "teaching" after it has mentioned making disciples and baptising (Matt. 28:17, 20). It is exegetically debatable whether Mathew's use of participles in these verses really allows such an understanding of the verses, for it may be argued that the participles actually refer to simultaneous activities. However, it is certainly true that conversion and baptism must lead into further instruction in the faith and further edification of the new Christian. But that does not negate the example of Jesus in so preaching and teaching that many were scandalised and put off from following him. We do not find him indulging in an activist search for ever increasing numbers of disciples at the expense of quality. So W. Scott (*Karl Barth's Theology of Mission*) says: "The church must be more concerned with quality than quantity." It is true therefore that what Dr. McGavran calls "the tremendous pressure to 'perfect' " (*How Churches Grow*) may, as he says, hinder numerical growth; but is that necessarily wrong?

Mark in his Gospel places great emphasis on the wilderness as the basis of the life of Jesus (e.g. Mark 1:3, 4, 12, 13). As O. Böcher demonstrates in the *New International Dictionary of New Testament Theology*, the wilderness in the Old Testament and New Testament

was not only a holy place in which God appeared to his
people, fed Elijah and all Israel in their desert wander-
ings, but it is also a place of "deadly danger" where
demonic powers hold sway (e.g. Deut. 8:15). "Post-bib-
lical Judaism . . . awaits the redemption of Israel from
the desert," and so Mark stresses the desert context of
John the Baptist and Jesus himself. The desert wander-
ings necessarily precede entry into the promised land;
the temptation in the wilderness introduces the coming
of the Kingdom and the ministry of Jesus. We today
dare not bypass the message of a costly wilderness experience when we invite men to enter the Kingdom and
become disciples of Jesus Christ. Discipleship is no bed
of roses.

Professor Lane in his commentary on Mark's Gospel
further points out that "the biblical concept of repentance, however, is deeply rooted in the wilderness
tradition". It was in the wilderness that Israel experienced "the period of true sonship" (Prof. Lane) and repentance unto life as God's adopted children therefore
necessitates a return to the realities of the wilderness.
There is a danger in shallow numbers-conscious evangelism that we entice people to become Christians with
promises of new satisfaction, joy, peace and love, but
we may fail not only to show them the harsh realities of
the wilderness, but also fail to emphasise the absolute
necessity of repentance in which we forsake the worldly
attitudes of the normal non-Christian. Prof. Lane describes this elegantly: "They return to a place of judgment, the wilderness, where the status of Israel as God's
beloved son must be re-established in the exchange of
pride for humility. The willingness to return to the

wilderness signifies the acknowledgement ... of dis-obedience and rebellion, and a desire to begin once more."

Depth of understanding in heart and mind at con-version prefaces a life of holy discipleship. God surely looks for a quality which cannot be plotted on statistical graphs. Some people may assure us that examining quantity will lead to assessing quality also. In practice quantity does not always necessarily reflect quality, nor does it always lead to the desired goal.

2 *"People movements"*

Many Christians in Third World countries have begun to object vociferously to what they consider the unduly individualistic religious concepts of western Christians. They accuse us of allowing pietism to blind our eyes to group approaches and therefore to the plural nouns and verbs of Scripture.

Some Latin American liberation theologians have seen an emphasis on changing the structures of society as the only alternative to pietistic conversion of indi-viduals. The Church Growth movement has rightly drawn our attention to the neglected possibility of group turnings to the Lord.

The early history of mission throughout Europe dem-onstrates the validity of such peoples' movements. Kings and tribal leaders accepted the Christian message and all their subjects followed them into baptism. Critics have rightly pointed out that there is an inherent danger of gross nominalism, for most of the people in such cases turn to the Christian faith purely in obedi-ence to their leaders without any question of repentance or realisation of the call to return to the "wilderness". But it should be pointed out that such turnings opened the way for the peoples of Europe to be instructed in the faith which they now professed.

It should be said that these early European peoples' movements stemmed from blind obedience to powerful sovereigns. Group turnings to Christ can be of a different nature.

In many cultures people think more collectively than individually. Tribes, villages or families act together and make decisions together. This can be so much an ingrained part of everyday life that it is almost inconceivable that an individual would make a private decision and act upon it independently of other people. This must of course influence decisions to follow Christ and abandon their old ways and religion.

In Indonesia my wife and I experienced the possibility of such group turnings. This was a new idea for us, but we saw that with good teaching and follow-up the results could be excellent. The first such turning that we ourselves witnessed was in a hospital ward. I had visited this ward and preached in it, leaving Christian literature for the patients to read and discuss together. When I returned to them the following week, they announced that they had decided to turn to the Lord. During the week they had read the literature, discussed and debated together until they came to a group decision to become Christians. This incident was not unique. Before we had arrived in Sumatra, a whole army regiment had together decided to follow Christ. After we left the country a senior school where we had had some influence agreed together to be baptised and follow the Lord. There were also many cases of families or sections of a village making group decisions for Christ.

In each of these Indonesian examples, the movement came as a result of democratic group decisions. This was not the sheep-like following of a weak crowd after a strong leader. David Wilkerson in his *The Cross and the Switchblade* describes his work with New York gangs. He shares how he always tried to win over the leaders of the gangs in order that all the other members might become Christians with the leader together. This has in it the danger of attracting weak nominal young people to the Church who may turn out to be lacking in true discipleship. On the other hand it obviates the problem of loneliness which can afflict such atypical Christians when they come into the Church. If they become Christians as a group they will have a sense of fellowship and solidarity which will give them an increased stability in their new life and faith.

David Wilkerson has certainly shown up a wrong approach which is sadly common amongst us. So often we aim our witness at the weak link in a gang or group, trying to wean them from their fellows. Of course it is true that Jesus came to save the weak and needy of this world, but we must not be surprised if such an approach to witness causes stronger members of society to despise us. Cowardly avoidance of the strong who form public opinion never characterised the apostles of Jesus himself.

In many societies one individual alone can hardly survive as a Christian. Islam decrees death for apostasy. The lonely martyr in a staunch Muslim land gives food for an inspiring book to be read by Christians in the comfort of their armchairs. But in such a situation the blood of the martyrs has not been the seed of the church. Islam has murdered one lone Christian after another in such lands as those of North Africa, but it has not given birth to churches. Martyrdom and persecution in places where the Church is already large and strong have led eventually to the growth of the Church, but not in areas where the Church is either very weak or actually nonexistent.

In such places we need to see groups of people turning to the Lord together. When working among Muslims in South Thailand I met the headman of a tiny village. He came each week to our mission hospital where I was working as evangelist. Over the weeks we became good friends and he invited me to visit his village. It was in an as yet unmapped area and very remote. I cycled through the tropical sunshine for several hours and eventually found this little community with its two hundred people. At my friend's invitation I explained the Gospel to all the people of the village, for he had called them together to meet me. Everybody in the village was related to the patriarchal figure of the headman.

After some time of questions and discussion I left them to trudge my cycle through the rough paths homewards. I never again returned to that village, for in my mind it was just one small place amongst hundreds of other little villages in the area, all of which were solidly Muslim. At that early stage in my missionary experience my eyes were not yet opened to the strategic importance of working for a group turning to the Lord in such a Muslim land. Having only had a westernised theological training, I was sadly ill-equipped for cross-cultural mission.

Clearly that village could have turned en bloc to the Lord under the leadership of the headman. They could then have developed as a Christian community in the midst of a sea of their Muslim fellow-countrymen. From such a base the good news of Christ could have penetrated the whole area.

Are such group movements possible in the individualistic society of the western world? Not in all sections of our society. But there are people who tend to think and act as groups together. We have already noted the example of rough gangs in New York; similar groupings of bored youngsters exist in many of our lands and they tend to move as a united body. This is equally true of some groups of working men. We can even talk of whole pits or factories being "moderate" or "radical". We long that the message of Christ should be the overriding influence in the collective thinking of such men. Ricci and DeNobili, the great Jesuit pioneers in China and India, worked to make the truths of the Christian faith permeate the whole of these societies. We today need to work in such a manner that Christ becomes the masses' leader. What a difference this would make to all our nations! During recent strikes in Britain the Archbishop of Canterbury called for a new spirit of love and service to replace selfishness and greed. Yes! But this will only come if the multitudes follow Jesus as Lord.

Can we aim at group conversions in Britain and other western countries? Perhaps it may be possible to discuss the Gospel with our fellow secretaries in the office or other similar groups of associates. So often boredom and disillusionment underlie the casual chatter about boy friends, clothes fashions or the latest film on TV. We may be able to suggest to them as a group that together we see whether Jesus Christ could not give us a new purpose and depth of love. Boredom and apathy could yield to true happiness as they try together this new adventure of following Jesus. If our witness is aimed at such a group movement, it will have to include at some stage open discussion with people as a group together.

Likewise with married couples we may aim at families coming to the Lord together. When a child or a wife becomes a Christian or at least is interested in the faith of Jesus Christ, it will be helpful to try and discuss with them as a family the possibility and desirability of them becoming Christians together.

Some Christians may prefer to avoid the use of the term "group movement", particularly in the highly individualistic democracy of America. They may rather choose two other terms, "peoples' movements" and "multi-individual choice". The former is sufficiently alien that it will hardly exacerbate controversy in our churches. 'Multi-individual choice" may sound horrible to non-American ears, but actually it describes aptly what can happen in such group decisions as we encountered in Indonesia. Whether it be in an army regiment, a senior school or a hospital ward, groups of people discuss and debate together until they come to a common mind. They then make a communal decision. This is normal practice in united families in our own countries. Husband, wife and children of relative maturity discuss family projects together until they come to a consensus of opinion; they then act as a family. Committees do the same. One member of the committee or of the family may have reservations about the decision, but in the face of otherwise unanimous agreement they will follow the others in the assurance that this is right. Only if they disagree radically will they opt out of the decision. So each individual plays a vital part in the group decision – it is in fact therefore a "multi-individual choice". Individualists need not feel too threatened!

3. *Models*

The great Chinese philosopher Confucius thought that the masses would follow the example of their leaders. He stressed the need to have noble and unselfish philosophers and scholars at the head of the government and civil service to show the people a wise and selfless model to emulate.

Chairman Mao was deeply influenced by many aspects of Confucian thought, including this idea that the best form of instruction is by means of ideal models. These will act as stimuli to draw people on towards the required goals. Mao's practice did not always match his theory, but his stated aim was government by example rather than by coercion. Like Confucius, he believed in the efficacy of academic learning of correct philosophical and political thought. This would mould the thinking of the nation's leaders at every level from the cadre to the Chairman himself. They in turn would inspire and instruct the ordinary people who would pattern their lives according to the model they saw exhibited before them by their leaders.

But Mao also inspired his people through individual model people. The great example was an oppressed peasant called Lei Feng, the symbol of struggle and re-education. In 1949 his village was liberated by the Maoist forces and Lei Feng was helped in many ways by the peasant revolutionary leader. Lei Feng at first prostrated himself before this young revolutionary with the words, "you are my saviour". The peasant however replied, "No, child, Chairman Mao and the Liberation Army are our saviours." Lei Feng saw the light and became a "selfless soldier seeking always to serve the people". Mao expected all good Chinese to see the horror of the past regime and follow the exemplary model of Lei Feng in a new life of service for the people.

Mao established models also in the sphere of daily work. He set up the agricultural commune of Ta-chai. Millions of Chinese and also foreign visitors went on pilgrimage to admire this model of peasant agriculture. All good Maoists were encouraged to become "Ta-chai men", meaning that they should devote themselves to communal agriculture for the good of the whole people. Later at the end of Mao's life the emphasis shifted from agriculture to industrial development. Western papers talked much of China's desire for "industrial progress". The Chinese talk more in pictorial language and they set up a new model. Ta-ching is an industrial complex in the north of China. This is the new model to be emulated – all good Chinese should be "Ta-ching men".

A further Maoist model speaks particularly vividly to Christians. The "Meal of Bitter Remembering" which is sometimes used in a manner reminiscent of the Christian sacrament speaks poignantly. Yu Jen in his article

"Aunt Liang's Dinner Party" describes such a celebration in which the peasant Aunt Liang entertains a group of urban students. "On the other side (of the room) a space was reserved for recalling the bitter past . . . There were some pictures and exhibits which compared their miserable life in the old society with the happy life in the new . . . The dinner was served – wild vegetable soup, steamed bran and husks! The students understood what this dinner meant at once. Aunt Liang looked around and said with deep emotion: 'Children, take and eat . . .' No sooner had she spoken than tears raced into her eyes and streamed down her cheeks. With so many bitter grievances recalled to her mind, she began to tell of her sufferings in the old society . . ."

Such ritual acts as a model, as Raymond Whitehead says in his *Love and Struggle in Mao's Thought*, to "recall the past and to affirm the revolutionary effort to move beyond those bitter days". One longs that Christian sacraments and other enacted models would jerk tears from our eyes and spontaneous rejoicing from our hearts and mouths.

The growth of God's church may be encouraged through the presentation of exemplary models before the eyes of the people. Success breeds success. Life engenders life.

Churches all over Britain have been stimulated and encouraged by the examples set by a few leading churches. Christians go on pilgrimage to these Christian "Meccas" and return to their own congregations with new ideas on evangelism, worship, fellowship or organisational structures. People engaged in specific ministries will visit parallel situations where the Lord has obviously been blessing. Thus one of my students has for some years been involved in inner-city work in London before coming to college for further training. As part of his training he therefore spent a month in a parallel situation in Bristol and then wrote up the results of his research there on church growth in that parish. Likewise people interested in visitation evangelism will visit other churches which have already been practising such ideas with evidence of the Lord's blessings. Of course there is a danger that we assume the Lord will bless us in identical manner if we adopt the same approaches, whereas in fact all systems and ideas need to be adapted to suit the local community and the people involved. But nevertheless we can learn much from Christian "models".

Leading Christian speakers also have to decide which invitations to accept and which to decline. Should they go to those churches and fellowships which "need" them most? Or should they throw their added weight behind churches which already vibrate with life and may be "models" which will influence more widely?

In Indonesia my wife and I were asked to be responsible for lay training and Bible teaching in some seventy-five congregations. Some of these churches vibrated with life, while others still awaited Prince Charming's kiss. It was clearly impossible for two new missionaries with inadequate language and no experience to fulfil such a task. Some priorities had to be established. Strategy and God's guidance were essential.

We could have rushed from one congregation to another to encourage the weak and shore up the crumbling ministries of the semi-dormant churches. We felt it wiser to concentrate on those churches which showed signs of real life to encourage them to develop still further. They would then act as models to stimulate the others.

At that stage of the history of the groups of churches we worked with there were no youth fellowships of any kind in any congregation. Children endured the tedium of rather dreary Sunday schools until they escaped at the age of twelve. There was then nothing for them until they graduated to the Sunday services and mid-week home Bible studies. No missionary could possibly found or run youth work in so many churches in such a wide area. The only possible strategy was to concentrate on one central church until its youth meeting shone as an example to others, prodding them with the exhortation: "Go and do thou likewise."

On arrival in the market town where we were based, we soon discovered that the many large villages in the neighbourhood hungered with open mouths for the message of Christ. "If anyone would come and preach to us, we would turn," we were often told. But no one had the vision for evangelism. We itched with the nagging temptation to do it ourselves. But it was better that local Christians should initiate and carry out such evangelism, for this could then act as a model to stimulate others to catch the same vision.

And so God worked it out. He inspired one local man to organise six evangelistic teams to plant churches in six near-by villages. "If they can do it, so can we," said the leaders of some other congregations. So the work of evangelism spread.

Many of us in the west are spending ourselves prop-

ping up dying concerns. Crumbling institutions need
our support lest they finally collapse. Might our energies
sometimes be better expended in further assisting those
movements which could act as models to others?

4. *Do methods matter?*

We have looked briefly at such strategic issues in Christian mission as whether we should aim fundamentally at
"winning the winnables". This led us to discuss the
placing of Christians in relationship to our goal of
growth in the church. We have attempted to face the
knotty problems of the relationship of mission strategy
to resistant segments of population, to "multi-individual
turnings" and to the use of "models" in mission. But in
stressing strategy the danger rears its head again that we
oust the sovereign Spirit from our thinking. As we conclude this chapter therefore, we remind ourselves that
God frequently cuts through the paltry machinations of
his servants and works in ways which we never considered. The foolishness of God is far wiser than all our
human wisdom. We need constantly to be reminded that
without him we can do nothing (John 15:5), that he is
the all-powerful Lord of Glory and that therefore it is
only *with him* that "all things are possible" (Matt.
19:26).

As puny men, we tend not only to become proud of
our own abilities and therefore to trust our own strategies almost without consideration of the purposes of
God. We also tend to become somewhat rigid in our
thinking, so that we affirm particular mission methodologies without the flexibility to adjust our thinking and
working to the needs of different situations.

Let us therefore remain constantly open to God's re-direction and correction of our methods. There *are* factors in evangelistic method which may affect the growth of God's church, but let us submit mere man-made strategies to the over-ruling and over-riding sovereignty of God.

5 FACTORS IN SOCIETY

The growth of the Church is dependent on three participants. Supremely God determines the course of history and of the development of his Church. But God in his grace has allowed free will to men and has decided to use his people as his instruments. It is indeed rare that God acts independently to build his Church without the participation of Christians as his agents. Not only does the growth of the Church depend on the obedience and loving service of God's covenant people; the world outside the Church may still prove unresponsive.

In this chapter therefore we want to look at some factors in society at large which may affect man's responsiveness or resistance to the message of the Gospel.

"Is the mass movement in Indonesia a work of the Spirit or just a result of social or economic movements?" some people have asked. The question assumes a dichotomy between the working of God's Spirit and the development of history. It is however a vital part of the Old Testament revelation that God is the author of history. He does not merely create the world and then leave it to its own devices in a deistic way. He sovereignly directs the course of world history. The Bible shows God continuously at the helm.

God directs the course of political, social or economic situations which may then result in people becoming more open to religious change and thus to the Christian faith. Changes in society can be as much God's instrument to prepare men for his Gospel as more directly evangelistic work.

1 *Political factors*

Political developments in a country may cause people to consider the option of Christianity. In some Communist countries (e.g. the Soviet Union) political dissatisfaction with the government has led many more thinking young people and educated men to question whether Christianity might offer a viable alternative to the existing system. Just as Marxism is often the obvious alternative to a right-wing capitalistic regime, so in the oppressive Marxist lands people will again be moved to look at the extreme opposite. Many "Marxists" in the west or in such countries as Chile and South Africa have actually little real understanding of Marxist philosophy. They adopt Marxism as a flag of opposition to the status quo. So likewise the young opponent to the Communist status quo in Eastern Europe may be attracted to the standard of the Christian Church without actually knowing in depth the content of biblical faith. However it is also true that nominal adherence offers the possibility of such people learning to become informed and dedicated believers. The young western revolutionary may study the philosophy of Marx and Lenin, thus becoming a genuine Marxist. Likewise the young religious adherent in the Soviet Union will study the Bible and come to love Jesus Christ as Saviour and Lord as well as accepting him for his political significance.

All over the world political factors are pushing people either towards or away from the Christian

Church. In Latin America the Roman Catholic Church was traditionally equated with the politics of the establishment, while in Britain the Protestant Churches have also been walking hand in hand with the upper and middle classes. In both cases therefore the poor and also the working classes have been pushed away from these churches into the fold of materialism, atheism or of other churches. Many students in African and Asian cities like Nairobi or Jakarta have associated the Christian message with the white face of colonialism. They easily reject the message of Christ because of their hatred of colonialism rather than because they cannot believe the actual content of the evangel. Many in post-colonial Africa have searched for a true sense of the African soul and have been attracted back to the primal religious roots of their forefathers before the white man came to disrupt the continent. Over the past decade or so this has been particularly marked in Zaire and in Chad, where persecution of Christians has at times erupted for this reason. As Christians we need to be specially sensitive to such feelings of national pride and adapt our mission methods accordingly.

Of course the Gospel may also become attractive because of its racial associations. The youth of some Jewish and Asian immigrant families in the west want to become Christians in order to escape the narrow confines of their traditional societies. The older generation of immigrants, in their insecurity, stick close together with strict adherence to traditional culture. The younger generation will be educated in Europe, will have white friends and want to become integrated members of the host society. The symbolic act which signifies this integration into the wider society is often baptism into the Christian Church.

Religion can also be a rallying standard for racial opposition to some other power. In Burma in past years the Karen tribe strongly resisted and disliked the majority Buddhist Burmese who ruled the land.Their own traditional primal religion seemed an inadequate expression of their opposition, for it could not compete with Buddhism. On the other hand Christianity offered them a major world faith to which they could rally. As a people they were also attracted to the content of the Christian faith, but it was often hard to distinguish the motives which brought them to Christ. Whatever the road which God used to introduce them to himself, it has led now to a strong and virile Church which has withstood years of isolation and opposition.

In such a situation where the Christian faith is the possible symbol of opposition to government, should the expatriate Christian worker align himself with government or opposition? The Church Growth movement with its strong emphasis on the "winnable" would surely say that God had opened the door to the Karen and therefore we should enter that door with boldness. There is truth in such a strategy. But in such cases we should not be surprised if governments cancel our visas!

Political and economic factors often lead to grave insecurity. Constant revolutions plague Latin America and Africa. Britain too jumps from crisis to crisis, leaving some people in doubt as to whether the country is governable. Political problems often walk hand in hand with deep economic suffering. The whole world with few exceptions lives with inflation hanging over it like

Damocles' sword. During the writer's time in Indonesia inflation ran at some 500 per cent a year with devastating social consequences. In Chile under Allende it rose to 1,000 per cent a year. Under such circumstances it becomes impossible to continue any normal business activities, for these depend on financial credit. Even in the western world our relatively minor inflationary spirals have led to real financial insecurities. People cannot guarantee their future comfort, for nest eggs crack and are consumed under the burning heat of rising prices. One solution lies in the philosophy of "eat, drink and be merry"; but that cannot disperse the underlying insecurity, for it fails to face up to the stark realities. When peaceful stability and satisfaction evade us in normal everyday life, we may be moved to search for a new anchor to hold our lives from aimless drifting.

As Christians we believe that Jesus Christ is the rock of our salvation. He does not shift his ground in unstable change, for he is the "same yesterday, today and for ever" (Heb. 13:8). The insecurity of our present society provides a unique opportunity to encourage people to find new confidence through him. Jesus Christ offers to men a solid foundation on which to build meaningful lives. The message of Christ gives people a new basis of security in situations of political and economic disorder.

2 *Educational change*
Paulo Freire in his books on educational theory has emphasised the use of the classroom for political teaching. Children, he says, should be made aware of their social position and of the realities of class warfare and

oppression, according to the Marxist analysis of society. He dubbed this educational approach "conscientisation".

Freire wanted purposely to use education to mould the thinking of young people. Marx also saw the educational system as a tool in the hands of the ruling class. When Mao came to power in China, he followed the Confucian pattern of using education to teach his people "right" thinking in the service of the people. Marx, Mao and Freire rightly saw the significance of education in shaping the lives of young people. We may query their use of the power and influence of education, but we cannot doubt their presupposition that education *does* have the ability to change attitudes in a nation.

In the past hundred years education has revolutionised many African societies. Tribal parents in isolated tight-knit communities have sent their children to schools in the towns. Here they have learned to know something of the wider world. They come to question the old culture and the old ways of life.

Europe went through this stage of development some years ago. New patterns of education made people think more critically. No longer were we satisfied with the traditional answer, "we've always done it this way and it's right". The question "why?" springs frequently to the lips. Many parts of the Third World today are facing precisely this situation. New forms of education make people ask questions and expect rational answers.

Higher education encourages people to ask fundamental questions. Who am I? What is the purpose of life? How can guilt be assuaged? How can society be improved? How can the nature of man be made less selfish? Such foundational questions demand answers. We dare not reply glibly to such heart-searching issues, but the faith of Jesus Christ does have much to say in response. Many Christians today are battling to formulate our faith on such questions. We want our Christian lives to relate to the basic needs of the modern day. But even if we have no simple solutions, we still believe that a true application of Scripture gives hope to students in their baffling search. The growth of the Church will depend partly on whether we can apply our faith intelligently to modern questions and whether we can influence the course of new educational trends.

The influence of educational thinking makes an immediate impact upon those of university or tertiary education level. Any change in the direction of the winds of philosophical thought affects the students' course. But it may take a generation or more for this to permeate through to the lower echelons of schooling. The new directions of thought influence the universities which in due course puff at the sails of teacher training establishments. They then shift the rudders of their student teachers who in their turn are launched on to the high seas of our schools. But they cannot immediately change the patterns of teaching or the content of a syllabus, for books and courses need to be written and published. For the future development and growth of the Church it is therefore vitally important that Christians penetrate the inner sanctums where educational thought and policy is determined.

So in Britain we now find young lads with hardly an O level to their names announcing that science has disproved religion and the Bible. Top scientists in space research and other circles may be less convinced of such an assertion! But the critical ideas of a past generation are now the common property of youngsters at school. Theological and educational battles in today's ivory towers will spill over into less rarefied atmospheres in the next generation. The decline or growth of the church of tomorrow depends on the currents in today's educational world.

3 *Cultural factors*

Networks of cultural or social relationships can speed or impede the spread of the Gospel. Those working for the growth of the Christian Church need to be aware of such family and social links.

(a) *Social relationships* In every form of society there are some people to whom we relate naturally and others who are separated from us by social barriers. People working in the same job together may form such a close relationship that they will readily hear the Gospel from one of their number. In some older areas of our cities there may still be a real sense of community which would allow the Gospel to spread naturally from one home to another. Most villages retain a nucleus of traditional village folk whose families have known each other and grown up together from generation to generation. The Gospel can run smoothly along the rails of such familiar relationships. The difficulty is the initial penetration of such groupings; but then it is relatively easy to spread the message of Christ from one to another within the group. So the church will grow by gathering whole networks of people into its fold. This is not a "multi-individual choice", for each individual makes a separate decision of faith and commitment. But the web of relationships facilitates the spread of the message.

On the other hand there can also be cultural and social barriers which hinder the natural communication of the Gospel from one person to his neighbour. Class distinctions make it hard for one man to hear what his colleague is seeking to tell him. Snobbery hardens the heart and makes the ear deaf to the witness of the Christian who is considered socially inferior. Likewise an inverted snobbery may hinder the working man from accepting the testimony of a Christian from the upper-middle classes. A local dialect or a posh Oxford accent can erect such walls of prejudice that it becomes hard to hear the word of the Lord.

Position and status in one's firm may also obstruct the natural flow of the Gospel from person to person. To follow the religious beliefs of one's employer may be considered either as betrayal of one's colleagues at work or as a means of ingratiating oneself with the boss for the sake of promotion. If the boss is a Christian, it may then be almost impossible for his employees to accept his witness and follow his faith.

The Church in any locality needs to evaluate the various networks of social relationships and then purposefully aim to break into as many of them as possible. Christians should ask themselves which people stand in such a relationship with them and therefore to whom they may most readily witness. It is unfortunate if the church fails to utilise such social factors in the spread of the Gospel, but allows people to disseminate the message widely without being aware of social realities.

When I was at university the Christian Union used to obtain a list of all new students at the beginning of each new academic year. This list included the home town of each student and the school from which he came.The Christians prayed over this list and then each Christian student volunteered to visit certain new students to invite them to an evangelistic coffee group. New students from public schools were visited by Christians from a public school. Students from Scotland found a fellow-Scot on their doorstep. Students doing modern languages soon found they had contact with a Christian student in the same academic field. Socially natural lines of communication were thus utilised as far as possible.

(b) *Family networks* Shearer points out in his Church Growth study on Korea that the rapid spread of the Gospel through many areas of that land came about largely through family links. The good news of Jesus Christ shot through the land along the arteries of family connections.

In many parts of the world the system of extended families still holds sway. Despite urbanisation and the consequent move towards narrowing families down to the western pattern of nuclear families, yet still in most Third World countries people feel a deep relationship with a multitude of relations. Aunts and uncles, cousins and second cousins abound. This causes problems socially in lands where nepotism flourishes, but for the spread of the Gospel it offers enormous opportunities. Once one member of a wide-spread family has been converted to Jesus Christ, the whole network of relations becomes easily reachable. The Church should therefore be encouraging all Christians to visit round their extended families to share their faith with them.

In some fast-changing societies parents and the older generations begin to feel their inadequacy in face of modern life. Whereas in the past they would have expected their children to follow them, now they wonder whether they should not be following the example of their children. I remember talking with a bewildered middle-aged couple in Indonesia. Their children had become followers of a variety of different faiths – Islam, Catholicism, Protestantism, Seventh Day Adventism, etc. They knew that their children were better adjusted to the modern world than they were, so they desired to believe the religion of their children. But they could not join so many faiths all at once! They asked me which I would recommend. I confess that my answer was not without bias!

Recently a young Pakistani Christian told me that her parents in Britain had asked her to introduce a Christian Christmas into their nominally Muslim home. They felt the need to adapt to their British environment and to the Christian faith of their daughter. So the Gospel moves along family lines.

In western society we have often lost the deeply united family feeling. Even first cousins hover on the edge of the family, while second cousins hardly enter our consideration. Nevertheless we do have opportunity to share our experience of Christ to those relations with whom we do have reasonably close contact. And the very fact that we are in their family gives the Gospel increased credibility. At college I am often encouraged to hear of students' parents, brothers and sisters who have come to Christ through a student. As these brothers and sisters get married the Gospel may then move into yet other families.

4 *Praeparatio Evangelii*

Some Christians in the past have so emphasised the pervasive horror of sin and the all-corrupting nature of original sin that they have seen conversion as a total break with the past. Life in Christ is totally new.

This emphasis, commonly called "discontinuity", has sometimes led to unloving and sweeping negative criticism of other faiths. It sometimes failed to see the remnants of the creational image of God in other religions and their adherents. Biblical theology has always insisted that the doctrine of total depravity does not deny the continued existence of some good and truth in man. It does however rightly teach that these remnants of truth are contaminated by the ubiquitous presence of sin. Now that which is good and true in the lives of non-Christians can be brought to fruition by the crowning glory of the Christian faith. So "continuity" as well as "discontinuity" play a vital role in Christian mission.

Many today have built upon the foundation laid by Stanley Jones long ago in his *The Christ of the Indian Road* (1925) which asserts that "wherever there is faith, it is reckoned unto them for righteousness". Tolstoy likewise said: "Where love is, God is." These have opened the door to the recent emphasis on dialogue. This has not only opposed the insensitive approach of monologue, which John Stott has also attacked in *Christian Mission in the Modern World*. It has also stressed that "the God and Father of our Lord Jesus Christ is present and at work" in the non-Christian, so that the aim of dialogue is "to meet Christ in him" (R. Hooker: *Outside the Camp*).

Professor John Hick in *Truth and Dialogue* understands things somewhat differently. He sees Christianity not as the climax and fulfilment of other religions, but on a par with them. All religions, he feels, have truth and validity for those who believe them, but they are actually all mere developments and expressions of some greater "ultimate divine reality". He therefore sees the aim of dialogue as a "fuller grasp of truth" in which "our present conflicting doctrines will be transcended". The evangelical Christian cannot accept this rejection of biblical and apostolic revelation and truth.

These views touch on today's major theological debate: is there revelation and salvation outside of the historical Jesus Christ? This enormous subject goes beyond our scope for this book and this chapter. But it cannot be totally evaded when discussing the presence of bridges to the Gospel.

The danger of excessive emphasis on the depravity of non-Christian life may be insensitive pride. On the other hand an excessive emphasis on continuity can lead to what Martin Buber in his *Schriften über das dialogische Prinzip* calls "a mutual relativisation of convictions" and a failure to witness to "what I have come to know about Jesus Christ" (Visser t'Hooft, *No Other Name*). It may fail to deal with elements of the demonic and of sin in other faiths, thus tending towards the dangers of syncretism. Truths must of course be "continued" when people are introduced to the full revelation of God in Jesus Christ. But unbiblical accretions to these truths will need to be countered through adequate and uncompromising biblical teaching. This is fundamental to the healthy life and growth of the Church.

(a) *A Muslim example* Let us illustrate this. The Muslim believes in Allah, the unique creator God. Allah is sovereignly all-powerful and far too great to take a wife and have a son in human fashion. The Christian is totally in agreement with these beliefs about God. They form an introduction to the fuller revelation of himself which God has granted us in the person of Jesus Christ and in his Scriptures. But we shall also have to counteract certain unbiblical emphases in these Islamic beliefs. In Islam the power of God may override his holiness and his love. Thus the Muslim dare not affirm that "God *must* fulfil his promises", or "God *must* keep his word", for this limits the sovereign power of Allah. The Christian doctrine of assurance of salvation and our certainty in prayer become almost blasphemous to the Muslim. Like a powerful Arab sheikh God may dispense mercy or judgment according to his fancy. The Quran constantly reminds us that God is merciful, so we may assume that he will often or even usually show mercy, but we cannot be absolutely sure. The Christian revelation of God differs radically from this. The Muslim also assumes that God's greatness prevents the possibility of God having a son. We agree that carnal sonship is impossible in the godhead, but the reality of the Trinity and of Jesus being the Son of God constitutes a vital part of the Christian faith. With the Muslim therefore there will be both continuity and discontinuity.

This applies equally to the normal irreligious westerner. He will have a vague belief in a remote power called "God", but his concept of the nature and work-ings of God will be both inadequate and also often er-roneous. Again there will be continuity and discontinuity. With the average Britisher therefore we shall still talk of "God", but shall need to teach more fully the true nature and character of God. Likewise in evangelism among the rough elements of some football supporters' clubs there will be considerable continuity. They stress a deep sense of community loyalty which may be fulfilled by the greater Christian truth of fellow-ship as the body of Christ. Their system of developing from young non-fighting supporters up to the higher levels of aggressive initiators of violence will require considerable change when they come to Christ; but in Christ too there is growth and development. Their sacrificial willingness to fight and sacrifice for the team they love makes some Christian discipleship look almost effeminate. Their total dedication to the cause is tragically misdirected, but it could be spiritually power-ful if Christ became their Lord.

In Britain and other western countries there has for some years been a steady trickle of people who have opted out of the rat-race of society. The lovelessness of depersonalised city life has moved some to emphasise caring and sharing in communal living. Words like "love" and "joy" characterise their highest aim as they seek for a form of life which is not dominated by selfish materialism. Acceptance of the Christian faith will necessitate a complete break with the wrong use of drugs and sex; biblical teaching will give a new content to "love" and other fundamental words, but there will also be a considerable degree of continuity as they find

Jesus Christ as the perfect fulfilment of their dreams.
(b) *An eastern example* So also with the modern young
person's application of the Hindu and Buddhist practice
of yoga and meditation which have become so popular
in the west today. The Christian will agree totally with
the need for a right disciplining of mind and body. We
agree with the need for peace in the midst of a turbulent
rat-race world and the Christian may be rebuked by
yoga practitioners, for we often allow ourselves to
become such feverish activists that we fail to enjoy the
peaceful luxury of quiet communion with God. But
Hindu philosophy stresses the unreality of the created
order, whereas the Christian is called upon to be world-
affirming and "in the world" even though not "of the
world". The Hindu in yogic practice seeks to lose self-
awareness in order to realise harmony of being. The
Christian believes in unity with God in a loving relationship, but we do not believe that meditation should aim at
the realisation that "we are not". God's great revelation
of his own nature was "I am" and we are called to be
like him.

Christian meditation therefore aims at a greater love
for the person of our God. We meditate on him, on his
amazing and gracious love for us. We seek so to relate to
him that we become more perfectly attuned to his purposes for us. He made us, he knows us and he has given
us our personalities with a purpose.

In summary, we rejoice in every evidence of truth,
good and beauty to be found in the non-Christian world.
We know that such remnants of the creational image of
God in man afford vital bridges for the introduction of
the Gospel of Christ which is the unique crown and

fulfilment of all that is good. But we are also aware that sin pervades every aspect of the nature of man and of the religions, so we are determined to resist the dangers of syncretism with the weapon of biblical teaching.

5 Social change

The Church Growth movement has put us in its debt by reminding us forcibly of the sociological fact that changes in society open people to new philosophies and religious views. The static society on the other hand results in minds that are closed to all that is new. Such generalisations are of course subject to the overruling sovereignty of the Spirit of God, who does from time to time work miraculously even in societies not subject to other great agents of change. But generally the Christian in his strategy for evangelism needs to be aware of the relative openness which usually results from social change.

(a) *In the individual* Every pastorally minded minister is aware of the significance of those major events which change the whole course of a person's life. Engagement and marriage often cause people to rethink their philosophy and life-style. They are likely to find themselves changing their circle of friends, for some of their unmarried friends will drop off while they will find themselves more drawn to other young married couples. No longer can they exist selfishly for themselves alone, for now there are two of them and they have to take each other into consideration in every decision. This will inevitably lead to some personality adjustments which can sometimes cause trauma. New joys and new problems are associated with new relationships.

This will go a stage further when the first baby comes. The young mother will probably have to give up her job with all the personal satisfaction and wider contacts it has given her. Her natural instincts may concentrate her affection on her baby with the danger that all else is excluded. Both parents now want the best for their child and may well wonder whether religion plays any part in this. That question will be underlined by the actual miracle of a baby's birth when a young mother's thoughts are often turned in a new way to God. Then also they may face the question of whether to have their baby baptised. Tradition and perhaps superstition will push them towards this, but they will then have to question the meaning of such a religious practice for them.

Sadly today a high proportion of marriages end up in divorce or in less than satisfactory relationships. The agony of such a situation will make many a heart cry for help and support. Is the Church aware of the crumbling of defences which this affords? Do we give the loving fellowship and support needed? Will such people find the Lord himself their comfort in the emptiness of life?

Serious sickness and suffering may also cause people to look for deeper meaning to life than mere materialism. Money and status have little to offer in the great crises of life. For some the experience of suffering will lead to a sad bitterness which twists the whole character. For others, weakness, suffering and sickness may prove the occasion when people realise that they are inadequate in themselves and need the loving power of God to sustain them.

Bereavement, too, takes us beyond the narrow confines of this life on earth to consider the great questions of eternity. The shock and loneliness of losing a loved one throw us into such disturbance that the whole direction of our lives has to be reshaped.

Not only the major events of life transfer us from one stage of life to another and thus give the opportunity to reconsider our whole purpose and direction. It is also the lesser changes in everyday life which can prepare us for entry into a new faith.

In our colleges and universities we know that first-year students are more open to consider the message of Jesus Christ than they will be when they have settled down into their new life. Most students who are converted find Christ in their very first term at college. Coming from home and school to the freedom of university with all its challenges forces us to open ourselves to new ideas. If the Christian Union wants to have a vital impact among their fellow students, it is vital that they make early contact with the new students.

Moving house will have some sort of impact. All the old roots are pulled up, so that we have no sense yet of belonging. A multitude of little jobs still need doing in the home and we feel the need of friendly neighbours to help. And we want to get into a new circle of friends in this new area. A warm-hearted church which makes early contact may find a ready response to its loving fellowship and practical help. So the Christian in an Estate Agent's office can contribute significantly to the Church's evangelism.

A new job can lead to a sense of deep insecurity. The question will often arise as to whether one can cope with the demands of the new situation. The world's facade of business-like efficiency slips only too easily. This gives the Christian the opportunity to make personal contact beyond the usual small-talk with which many people mask their thoughts. Personal relationships at a deeper level allow us to share the Christian confidence in an ever-present Saviour who is our help, our strength and our companion.

Every change in our personal situations makes us more open to new influences, including the witness of the Christian.

(b) *In society* As people we are caught up in the great movements of society today. And just as we are made more receptive by changes in our personal lives, so also we are affected by sociological change.

i *Urbanisation* All over the world urbanisation proceeds apace. Statistics of city growth have become so common that they bore us. Likewise much paper and ink are devoted to descriptions of the sociological problems inherent in such massive and rapid urban development. What our sociologists are saying also relates to the evangelistic task of the churches. New city dwellers are open to new ideas. Cut off from the restraints of traditional close-knit communities, people are free to adopt new political and religious affiliations. Separated from all their previous friends and family, they will make new connections in the city.

Ivan Vallier in *Catholicism, Social Control, and Modernisation in Latin America* sees that Latin American societies are "involved in a critical transition stage between tradition and modernity". Gustavo Ramirez, writing in John Considine's *The Religious Dimension in the New Latin America* notes that in the United States "Americans are turning increasingly to their religious groups . . . for the satisfaction of their need for communal identification and belongingness"; so he argues that urbanisation does not necessarily result in a break with religion. But he does see that "the trek to the cities creates a religious crisis", which in Latin America largely means a loosening of ties to the Catholic Church and an openness to Marxism and Pentecostalism.

Gino Germani, writing in *Latin America – the Dynamics of Social Change*, also emphasises that "the new urban sectors" may "originate new political forces often threatening the social and political status quo". This of course applies equally to the religious status quo. But sociologists also point out that in Britain, as in other countries, the new urban dweller gradually settles down into new established social, political and religious patterns. From a Christian point of view therefore, we may say that he will be relatively open to the Gospel of Jesus Christ for the first few years of his life in the big city, but after that he will become increasingly resistant. He will have established new friends and a new way of life, which the Gospel would gravely disturb. Evangelism needs to concentrate primarily, although not exclusively, on those who have recently transferred to a city.

ii *Weak and strong cultures* At different stages of history various groupings of people have lost confidence in the vitality and validity of their own culture. In direct contact with some other apparently superior or stronger culture they become susceptible to radical change.

In the early days of white incursion into the continent of Africa some tribes resisted strongly, for they maintained a genuine pride in their own civilisation. They did not consider their culture in any way inferior to that of the white peoples. But other tribes had been decimated by inter-tribal warfare and by the ravages of the slave trade, so that they had become imbued with a deep sense of their own inferiority. When the white man came they were impressed by his apparent religious and cultural strength. The whites also gave out an air of proud confidence. In such circumstances these particular tribes happily embraced the religion of the European, although many did not greatly understand what this involved.

In the Old Testament we find the same situation. It was an accepted practice that peoples should adopt the religion and the gods of a conquering nation. When King Ahaz became a vassal of Assyria, he saw the heathen altar in Damascus and caused Urijah the priest to make for the Jerusalem Temple an altar of the same "pattern, exact in all its details" (2 Kings 16:10). The supremacy of a nation implied the superior power of its gods.

A few years ago I visited the Karen tribe in North Thailand. Many of this tribe suffered tragic half-lives under the influence of opium. The whole culture seemed to totter with despairing demoralisation. With humiliating respectfulness they looked up to the seemingly superior culture of the Thai. In such circumstances it was inevitable that Buddhism, the religion of the Thai people, should hold great attraction for the Karen.

iii *Wide religious contact* A few years ago my wife and I were asked to help at a Christian houseparty in Britain for overseas students. Here we met a Turkish student doing his Ph.D in a British university. He told us his story.

As a child he was brought up in a remote Turkish village by his devout Muslim grandmother. She taught him that Mohammed is the "seal of the prophets", the final and perfect climax to a long line of prophets sent by God through the ages. He came to believe implicitly that Christianity and Judaism have corrupted the divine Books sent to them by God through their prophets, so that today there is only the Quran in existence. Jews and Christians have developed blasphemous teachings which even suggest that there are three gods – God the Father, Mary his wife and Jesus their son. Other religions are even worse with their gross idolatries. Only Muslims, he was taught, are pure and holy in truly following the revelation of the One God.

Then our friend went to the city to study at the university. Here he lived in a hostel with all sorts of other students. Most were at least nominally Muslim, but a small minority were Christians. He commented to us as he relived his amazement of those days, "They weren't any worse than us Muslims." This realization that Christians could be no worse than Muslims revolutionised his whole view of religion. He came to ask himself whether Islam is indeed the final and only true religion. He wondered whether Christianity might even be considered a valid faith. And so he came to our houseparty. Wider contact with non-Muslims made him more open to consider Christianity as a viable option. This of course applies equally to British Christians, if they meet sincere, moral followers of other faiths. They may come to doubt the uniqueness of Jesus as the one Saviour for all men.

Dr. McGavran in his early book, *Church Growth in Mexico*, points out that migrant workers from Mexico to the United States often come into vital contact with Protestant churches. This widening religious experience forces them to reconsider whether their traditional Catholic faith is true and right. They then become more open to the preaching of a biblical message of Jesus Christ by Protestants.

The same applies to young people in Britain who are brought up in narrow communities and then break out into the wider world. Young Jews and other immigrant young people inevitably come face to face with other philosophies and religions when they emerge from their ghetto cocoons. For some this will prove to be a "mind-blowing experience" which will prepare them to welcome the Gospel of Christ.

Likewise many a youngster from a typically British irreligious or nominally Christian home is made receptive to new ideas by contact with the wide spectrum of religious life in the city or at university. Here he meets fellow students who indulge in all the various religions of the world. The mysterious and frightening reality of the occult makes him aware of powers in the supernatural realm. Inevitably he wonders what is right and true. At home he sailed smoothly through life without being confronted by spiritual realities, but now he is forced to question his old traditional forms of religion. The vibrant testimony of living Christians now becomes relevant to his situation: formerly it would have been felt to be fanatical.

Conclusion

Believing in the God who determines the movements of history and society, the Christian should have his eyes wide open to see what God is doing to prepare men for the reception of his Gospel. As a result of God's working in history different races and strata of society will become more open to the Gospel at different times. Let us pray with renewed urgency and faith that "God may open to us a door for the Word" (Col. 4:3).

The Christian needs to be aware of movements in society and adjust his witness and the emphasis of his church to reap the harvest which God offers us.

6 YOU IN YOUR SMALL CORNER

Christians today are encouraged by a barrage of statistics which demonstrate what Karl Barth in *Church Dogmatics* called the Church's "astonishing capacity for numerical increase". We have been impressed by the mushrooming growth of Chilean and Brazilian Pentecostal churches, by the evangelical churches of West Africa and the Anglican churches in the east of that continent. Stories of revival in Indonesia have sometimes been exaggerated, but nevertheless all of us are impressed by the fire which lies behind the smokescreen of sensationalism. In South Korea too Dr. Joon Gon Kim in his Asian Perspective Pamphlet No. 17 talks of the founding of six new churches every day in that land. He asserts that from 1974–78 "Christians were added to the Korean Church at an average rate of 1 million per year." We know that such statistics are notoriously unreliable and also that they do not and cannot tell us of the quality of discipleship amongst these new believers; but in spite of that we are impressed by the rapid growth of the Church in many areas of our world today.

We are encouraged too by the beginnings of a new upturn in many European churches. The days of steady decline and discouragement seem to be over. In the past we heard about God's workings overseas, but such movements of the Spirit seemed a far cry from our stagnant European situation. Until very recently (see

*Churches & Churchgoers in Patterns of Church Growth
in the British Isles since 1700* by Currie, Gilbert and
Horsley) all British Protestant denominations have
shown a continual reduction of membership. But today
life stirs also in European veins.

Some of us may question what we can do to encourage the growth of our church. If we belong to one of
the lively growing churches of our country, then we feel
ourselves to be a part of God's overall strategy for the
growth of the Church. We are in a moving ship and
sense the exciting throb of the engines thrusting us for-
wards. In such a church it is a joy to play our small part
according to our gifts in fellowship with all the other
members.

But what about the lonely Christian in a church
which lacks the pulsating life of the Spirit? What can we
do if the leaders of our church have not the vision of
growth and expansion which a relevant church can
often experience in the searching world of our day? Can
we expect God to work when our congregation is largely
elderly and does not relate to the cultural need of the
more receptive younger generation? Can we play a part
when we are perhaps students with no influence on the
leaders in the church?

A Chinese Christian friend of ours joined a rather
liberal Methodist church in Singapore. After a while he
volunteered to teach in the Sunday school and began to
share his faith with the other Sunday school teachers.
One by one they came to a living faith in Jesus Christ
until his goal was achieved – all the Sunday school
teaching was now in the hands of live Christians. By this
time our friend was appointed to be Superintendent of

the Sunday school and had also become a member of the Church Board. He persuaded the Board to allow him to start two new adult Bible classes, for which he invited two missionaries as teachers. One by one many people came to faith in Christ and the church was transformed despite the fearful lack of biblical exposition from the pulpit on a Sunday. The minister was not altogether sympathetic to evangelical doctrine and did not encourage the experience of personal conversion, but through one ordinary lay member God changed the whole character of that congregation.

A newly converted young university student in Britain belonged to a church where the ministry was not very evangelical. He joined the Youth Fellowship whenever he was home for his vacations. Being only an occasional visitor to the church and having no influence on the leaders, he began to pray that two local people would be converted through him. He asked the Lord for one local lad and one local girl to come to faith in Christ. God answered that prayer. Each week these two teenagers came to the student's home for Bible study and prayer to help them grow in their new-found faith.

God used those two young people. They led others to Christ. They taught in the Sunday school and then began a Pathfinder class for youngsters aged 11–15. As the years passed, these young Christians began to influence the Mens' Fellowship and the Young Wives Group. They led the work among the young people.

The church began to change, but what about the vicar? Would God answer prayer for him too? Whenever he preached a helpfully biblical sermon, these young Christians thanked him warmly. When his sermon failed to feed the congregation from the Word of God, then they merely greeted him warmly at the end of the service but did not mention the sermon. He began to notice what sort of sermon was well received.

Then God stepped in and changed his whole understanding of Christian truth. A young nurse came to faith in Christ, but had never been baptised as a baby. She of course asked to be baptised. The vicar's doctrine of baptismal regeneration did not fit this sort of situation. If without baptism she was still unregenerate, how could one explain the obvious change in her life? And if she was unregenerate, how could she now love the Lord Jesus and so want to be baptised? He was forced to rethink his doctrine of baptism and of regeneration.

Many a student dreads the vacation when he will have to leave the warm fellowship and lively Bible teaching of his Christian Union. He wonders how he will survive spiritually in the cool climate of his home church. Towards the end of the summer term students' prayers begin to beseech God to give them strength to persevere in love and faith through the four months at home! They forget that after leaving university they may have to exist for many years in such situations!

Many students and young people become easily frustrated because they cannot change a church overnight. They long to be able to influence the minister and other leaders, but realise that this is unrealistic. They are only young people with little experience, so the adult leadership of many churches will not pay great attention to them.

But patience is a virtue! God himself took centuries to prepare Israel for the coming of the Messiah. And since then he has already waited patiently for a further two thousand years while the church fulfils her mandate to evangelise the world, for "the gospel must first be preached to all nations" (Mark 13:10): only then will the Kingdom come to its climax with the glorious coming again of Jesus Christ.

Surely then we can afford to show a little patience in our longing to bring fire and life to our churches! By personal witness to one person after another we can have a great influence. And when we have had the privilege of leading someone to the Saviour, let us share with them right away our vision for the growth of our local church and also the growth of the Church worldwide.

However insignificant and relatively ungifted we may feel ourselves to be, all of us can and should have a contributory part to play in the extension and up-building of the Church. Some years ago I was challenged by the example of a young girl in her late teens. Of rather meagre education and being physically handicapped, she was aware that she could never be an outstanding leader in the Church. She had been brought up by an old grandmother in a narrowly sheltered environment. Rarely was she allowed to make friends with children of her own age when she was at school, so she grew up with the outlook and speech of an old lady. "I can't do much for the Lord," she said once, "but I try to befriend one person every year and help them to know the Saviour too." God helped her in this endeavour and used her to introduce one person each year to Jesus Christ.

God in his grace has granted to most of us more talents to use for him than he gave that girl. "Every one to

whom much is given, of him will much be required"
(Luke 12:48). All of us should ask ourselves, "What
aims do I have for the growth of the Church in numbers
and in quality?" But some of us are privileged to have
greater responsibility in the life of the Church. We may
have influence at various levels – in the leadership of a
congregation, in some youth work, in a house meeting
or with children. Let us re-examine some of the issues
raised in this book and ask ourselves what we can do to
help in the development of God's Church in our own
area and worldwide. Will God use us to help revitalise
the internal life of his Church? Or are there basic structural reforms which require to be made in the whole
organisation of the congregation? Do we need to rethink
the evangelistic methodology we use? And perhaps we
should look again at the society in which we are called to
live and witness as salt and light. Is our church relating
to current movements in our environment? Dr. David
Wells in *The Search for Salvation* says that our basic
task "is not so much that of finding new truth in the
Bible, but of finding new ways of making it truth for *our
world*."

It is significant also that the apostles in Acts 6 linked
prayer inseparably with their call to the work of preaching and teaching. "We will devote ourselves to prayer
and to the ministry of the Word" (Acts 6:4). Ministries
of evangelism and edification of God's Church need to
be firmly rooted in prayer. The old Rabbi Jose
b.Halafta said: "Nothing is greater than the power of
prayer."

As we conclude, we remind ourselves again that the
numerical growth and the sanctification of God's people

are both the work of the Holy Spirit. The Acts of the Apostles shows the Spirit to be both the initiator and the performer of everything associated with the growth and development of the church. He is the giver of life. As we rejoice in the glorious fact of the Spirit indwelling us, we are also humbled by the further truth that he works through us for the growth of the Church. In our service of the Lord, his Church and the world we are therefore utterly dependent on the gracious power of the Holy Spirit.

"You shall receive power when the Holy Spirit has come upon you; and you shall be my witnesses . . . to the end of the earth" (Acts 1:8).

RECOMMENDED READING

R. Allen: *Missionary Methods, St. Paul's or Ours?* World Dominion Press, 1912

D. Bentley-Taylor: *The Weathercock's Reward*, O.M.F., 1967

J. Blauw: *The Missionary Nature of the Church*, Lutterworth, 1962

H. Boer: *Pentecost and Missions*, Lutterworth, 1961

O. Costas: *The Church and its Mission*, Tyndale House, 1974

Currie, Gilbert and Horsley: *Churches and Church-goers: Patterns of Church Growth in the British Isles since 1700*, Oxford: Clarendon Press, 1977

R. De Ridder: *Discipling the Nations*, Baker Book House, 1971

E. Goldsmith: *God can be Trusted*, O.M.F., 1978

M. Goldsmith: *Don't Just Stand There*, I.V.P., 1976

M. Green: *Evangelism in the Early Church*, Hodder and Stoughton, 1970

V. t'Hooft: *No Other Name*, S.C.M., 1963

D. McGavran: *How Churches Grow*, World Dominion Press, 1959

D. McGavran: *Understanding Church Growth*, Eerdmans, 1970

(See also the various area studies of Church Growth published by Carey Press)

S. Neill: *History of Christian Missions*, Penguin Books, 1964

Pope Paul VI: *Evangelization in the Modern World*, Catholic Truth Society, 1975

W. Scott: *Karl Barth's Theology of Mission*, Paternoster, 1978

Explaining the Gospel in Today's World – Church Planting; Gospel and Culture, Scripture Union, 1978

J. Stott: *Christian Mission in the Modern World*, Falcon, 1975

D. Wells: *The Search for Salvation*, I.V.P., 1978

I BELIEVE IN THE CHURCH

David Watson

'NEW forms of worship, new experiments in communal living, new structures of lay ministry, new understandings of the nature of the Church have been flowering in Evangelical circles. And nowhere more than in York, where David Watson exercises a ministry which spreads far wider than the city and neighbourhood. He is well known as a missioner and preacher. What may well prove to be a far more significant contribution to Christianity in the twentieth century is the fact that he has rediscovered the dying art of church building: not in bricks and mortar, but in lives.

'**You will be staggered at the revolutionary impact of a Christianity which is radical enough to get back to the New Testament, and courageous enough to apply it in practice.**'

– from the Preface by Michael Green

'Who could not be genuinely moved, profoundly challenged and positively inspired by so *prophetic* a book as *I Believe in the Church*? . . . An urgent tract for the immediate present, and as such it must be read – *now*!'

Church of England Newspaper

I BELIEVE IN EVANGELISM

David Watson

'Fresh, lively and enjoyable ... solid thinking and practical application.'

Baptist Times

The revolutionary story of David Watson's ministry in York has captured the attention of press and television. Internationally renowed as an evangelist, he has been described as one of Britain's finest preachers. From his experience in a parish church, from university missions at home and overseas, he has written this major volume on evangelism which reveals the passionate convictions which motivate his ministry.

'Extremely important ... well written and cogently argued.'

Bishop Cuthbert Bardsley

WHY BOTHER WITH JESUS?

Michael Green

'Why bother?' considers Michael Green, is a widespread disease. Nothing seems to matter any more so long as we have our rise in wages, so long as the cost of our comforts is not too high, so long as we have a colour telly.

The disease has taken hold of our concern for the truth. When matters of right and wrong are settled by head-count rather than principle, a moral collapse could well be in the offing.

From this grim diagnosis Michael Green asks 'Why Bother With Jesus?', looking in detail at the qualities in Jesus which make us want to learn more about him.

Michael Green, Rector of St. Aldate's, Oxford, is author of *You Must Be Joking, New Life, New Lifestyle, I Believe in the Holy Spirit* and *Evangelism in the Early Church.*